THE HISTORY AND ARCHITECTURE OF BRIGHTON

THE HISTORY AND ARCHITECTURE OF BRIGHTON

by

ANTONY DALE

with a new foreword
by
the author

Republished S.R. Publishers Ltd., 1972
First published Brighton, 1950

Republished 1972 by S.R. Publishers Limited,
East Ardsley, Wakefield,
Yorkshire, England,
by kind permission of the author

ISBN 0 85409 740 6

Please address all enquiries to S.R. Publishers Ltd.
(address as above)

Reprinted by Scolar Press Ltd.,
Menston, Yorkshire, U.K.

FOREWORD

When this book was written in 1950 no satisfactory comprehensive history of Brighton existed. The two principal authorities were Eredge's "History of Brighthelmston" (1862) and Bishop's "A Peep into the Past: Brighton in the Olden Time" (1880). But both were long out of print and in any case suffered from the maddening defects of local history books written in the nineteenth century. They were totally lacking in system, chronology, or index. In more recent times several books appeared which dealt with a single aspect of Brighton's history: George Aitchison's "Unknown Brighton" with the lanes; H. D. Roberts's "The Royal Pavilion" with that building; Lewis Melville's "Brighton, Its History, Its Follies and Its Fashions" and Sir Osbert Sitwell and Margaret Barton's "Brighton" both with the occupants of the Royal Pavilion; and my own "Fashionable Brighton" with the principal squares and crescents. The first edition of the present book was an attempt to give a short account in one cover of all aspects of Brighton's history that were of interest. Since then Clifford Musgrave's "Life in Brighton" has been published which covers the ground much more fully and brings the story right up to date. But there is still room for a reprinting of this less detailed study.

In the 21 years since the first edition of the book appeared Brighton, like all historic towns, has had to suffer the assaults of modern development. In some places like Guildford and Gloucester these have been so destructive that the historic character of the place has been largely overlaid. Brighton has been more fortunate. It is true that whole areas have been cleared, but these were relatively deficient in interesting buildings. There has been the usual crop of tall new buildings, some of them in unsuitable places. The tower of St. Paul's Church, which used to be one of the most prominent features of the sky-line, is now dwarfed between two monsters. The new Royal Sussex County Hospital appears above the west side of Lewes Crescent. But by and large the town retains its Regency character. To achieve this has been a constant struggle on the part of the Regency Society and the other bodies interested in preservation. The major losses have been the Bedford Hotel, designed by Thomas Cooper in 1829, which burned down in 1964; St. Margaret's Church, one of the two best classical churches in the town, which was demolished as redundant by the Chichester Diocesan Finance Board in 1959; the Venetian Gothic Blind School of 1865 by Somers Clarke which had to make way for the new Latilla Institute of the Royal Sussex County Hospital in 1957; Grenville Place, which was quite unnecessarily included in the new Churchill Square development; and the Regency Gothic National Schools of 1830 in Church Street which Brighton Corporation laid low in 1971 without fulfilling the normal processes of consultation. But perhaps one of the worst blows to the general character of the town was the erection in 1964 along Marine Parade of exceptionally ugly lamp standards which now ruin any attempt to photograph Brighton's "royal mile." At the present time (1972) the West Pier, which is probably the oldest and most interesting pier in England, and the Attree Villa, recently the Xaverian College, which is one of the earliest examples of Italianate architecture in England, are under threat. If Brighton is to remain one of England's principal historic towns it is essential that demolitions in future should be limited to those buildings which are not of architectural or historic value and that new tall buildings are not allowed to upset the proportions of the general scene.

Before the foundation of the Victorian Society in 1957 the qualities of nineteenth century buildings were greatly undervalued. In Brighton, attention did not extend beyond the Regency. We now realise that the town contains a great deal of interest which dates from the late nineteenth century: an unrivalled series of churches, two piers and the Aquarium. These now need as much protection as the earlier buildings as they will be progressively under threat as the years pass.

ANTONY DALE
1972

CORRIGENDA

Page 18, line 13	Dr. Russell's portrait, here attributed to Zoffany, is now thought to be by Benjamin Wilson.
Page 23, lines 30 and 32	Both these street vendors have vanished from the scene.
Page 28, line 32	Sherrys Dance Hall has since been replaced by a fun fair.
Page 33, line 10	No. 12 Brighton Place was demolished in 1963.
Page 34, line 10	St. Stephen's Church is now used as a Deaf and Dumb Institute.
Page 35, line 15	The interior of Marlborough House has been much improved by redecoration and the removal of the partitions.
Page 36, line 11	This date should be 1804, not 1801.
Page 47, line 23	This is a mistake. Lord Barrymore's feat was performed at Mrs. Fitzherbert's earlier Brighton house.
Page 52, line 25	With modern prices this furniture would fetch infinitely more than half a million pounds.
Page 54, line 15	On the death of the last Miss Cowley the Old Bun Shoppe ceased to be a baker's, and the original shop front has been rebuilt with disastrous results.
Page 54, line 17	Andrew's Cottage has now reverted to use as a shop and is occupied by C. J. Carter & Co., Tailors.
Page 57, line 4	St. Margaret's Church was demolished in 1959.
Page 65, line 1	This derogatory view of the Town Hall needs revision. Although it has not been

completed to the original design it has considerable dignity and a very fine staircase. As the Bedford Hotel has been demolished it is now the only surviving known work of the local architect, Thomas Cooper.

Page 71, line 11	Brighton Corporation has now restored and maintains the Kemp Town Slopes.
Page 72, line 7	William Attree is a mistake. It should be Thomas Attree.
Page 72, line 13	The Xaverian College has now moved elsewhere. The house was saved from immediate demolition by a preservation order imposed by the then Ministry of Housing and Local Government but subsequently was scandalously neglected by the owners at that time. It is now empty and decaying, and the problem of its preservation remains to be solved.
Page 72, line 23	No. 1 Eastern Terrace (the Court Royal Hotel) has been converted into flats, and the staircase has been destroyed.
Page 80, line 15	This view has been modified by time. The West and Palace Piers have become objects of considerable interest both architecturally and historically.
Page 81, line 5	This brass plate has since been removed.
Page 82, line 28	Hooper Struve Limited have since given up their lease of the building. The owners, Brighton Corporation, wished to demolish it but were refused listed building consent to do so by the Department of the Environment. Its restoration and use are now under consideration.
Page 84, line 11	The Bedford Hotel was burned down in 1964.

THE HISTORY AND ARCHITECTURE OF BRIGHTON

By the same Author

JAMES WYATT, ARCHITECT, 1746-1813

FASHIONABLE BRIGHTON, 1820-1860

1 REGENCY SQUARE, NORTH SIDE

THE HISTORY AND ARCHITECTURE OF

BRIGHTON

by

ANTONY DALE

BREDON & HEGINBOTHOM LTD.
10 EAST STREET, BRIGHTON

FIRST PUBLISHED IN 1950

PRINTED IN GREAT BRITAIN
AT THE DOLPHIN PRESS LTD., BRIGHTON

CONTENTS

ILLUSTRATIONS

ILLUSTRATIONS—*continued*

Plate

ACKNOWLEDGMENTS

For permission to use the photographs in this book, the publishers wish to make grateful acknowledgment to the following:

THE NATIONAL BUILDINGS RECORD
for Plates 9, 10, 20, 21, 24, 28, 30 and 32

Miss R. E. ORMEROD for Plates 23 and 29

Mr. J. F. SMITH for Plates 1, 2, 3, 8, 16, 17, 18, 22 and 33

THE TIMES for Plates 15 and 25

Mr. K. J. BREDON for Plates 4 and 31

The map was drawn by K. J. CARR

CHAPTER ONE

The Fishing Village of Brighthelmston

THE EARLIEST human settlement within the area now covered by the County Borough of Brighton was on Whitehawk Hill, immediately to the south of the Grand Stand of the present Race-course. This was a Neolithic camp which was excavated by the Brighton and Hove Archaeological Society in 1929, in 1932-3 and in 1935. Two complete skeletons of women, one buried with her newly-born child, were found in 1929; and in 1935 skeletons of an adult male and of a child. The excavations also revealed a large quantity of fragments of human bones, found amidst animal bones and in close proximity to the remains of a fire, some of the bones even charred, from which it is difficult to avoid the inference that the inhabitants of 'the Brighton of Abraham's day', as it has been called, were cannibals. Another hill fort within the modern area of Brighton was on Hollingbury Hill. But this was not built until much later: about 250 B.C. against the threat of Marnian invaders who are known to have entered Sussex in the Worthing area. This was excavated by the Brighton and Hove Archaeological Society in 1931. To the west, on the site of what is to-day Palmeira Avenue, Hove, was a large tumulus or mound which, when excavated in 1857, was found to contain a Bronze Age grave. This mound, until levelled at that date, was so prominent a feature of the landscape that it actually gave its name to Brighton's sister town. Hoove, as Hove was first pronounced, is of Scandinavian derivation and denotes a mound. This tumulus contained a number of objects of which the finest was a cup known as the Amber Cup, now one of the most important exhibits in the Brighton Museum.

The origin of the name Brighthelmston, as Brighton was first called, is lost in the mists of time. It has been suggested by antiquaries that the name derives from a British word 'brist' or 'briz' meaning divided and refers to the fact that the village was once divided by a stream. The more romantic theory is that it was the 'tun' or town of a certain mythical Brighthelm, sometimes alleged to be a Saxon saint. If this is the case, it is probably not more far-fetched than any other theory to suggest, as Mr. George Aitchison has done in his book *Unknown Brighton*, that this eponymous hero's name made allusion to his shining headdress. The simplest theories are not always the least likely.

Of actual historical figures the earliest recorded in local annals is Ulnoth or Wolnoth, father of Earl Godwin, who held Brighthelmston at the time of Ethelred II, the Unready. From him the land descended to Godwin. On Godwin's banishment, it was taken by Edward the Confessor into his own possession and thence, on Edward's death, reverted to Harold, son of Godwin. The Conqueror granted Brighthelmston as part of the barony of Lewes to William de Warrenne, husband of Gundrada, who is now thought not to have been the Conqueror's daughter. At the time of the Domesday survey in 1081, the land comprised three manors: Brighthelmston-Michelham, Brighthelmston-Lewes, and Atlingworth, meaning in Saxon 'the home of the son of the nobleman', a name still perpetuated by the road called Atlingworth Street.

Of the earliest Brighthelmston not a trace survives to-day. It was built below the cliffs, as is the old part of Dover still extant, and was gradually swallowed up by the sea. Between 1260 and 1340 as much as 40 acres of land are said to have been submerged. But even as late as the beginning of the eighteenth century, long after the second Brighthelmston had been built above the cliffs, there were still 113 habitations occupied by fishermen below the cliff. These were destroyed during two furious storms in 1703 and 1705 respectively, when all the remaining houses below the cliff were entirely obliterated beneath a mound of beach.

The Upper Town, or the second Brighthelmston, was begun during the fourteenth century with the construction of East Street and West Street, to which North Street was added slightly later. When the two towns first co-existed, the Lower Town was principally occupied by fishermen, the Upper by landsmen. As the number of the latter grew, the intervening space between East and West Streets began to be covered with dwellings. Most of the ground now occupied by Black Lion Street and Ship Street was known as the Hempshares after the plots which it contained for the production of hemp to make ropes for the fishermen. The names of both these streets derived from inns on the site. The Black Lion having become a private house at the beginning of the nineteenth century and having subsequently been demolished, the Ship, since 1650 designated as the Old Ship to differentiate it from a newer establishment, is thus the oldest hostelry of the town. The rectangle of the Upper Town was completed by South Street long since claimed by the sea like the Lower Town below the cliffs.

The social, though not the geographical, centre of this medieval rectangle was the open space now known as Brighton Place, then called the Knab—another word of Scandinavian origin meaning a hill. Here were the town well and the meeting-place of the local townsfolk. To the south-west of the Knab, roughly in the angle of Market Street and Prince Albert Street, stood a Chantry or free chapel dedicated to St. Bartholomew, erected before the end of the thirteenth century, to which was attached a monastic grange or farm. This was an offshoot of the great Cluniac Priory of St. Pancras at Lewes and was served by two or three resident monks. The Chapel was destroyed by fire when the French burned the town in 1514, and it never recovered its former use or influence. At the Reformation, almshouses were built on the site. These were sold to the town in 1733 for £17 and converted into the Parish Workhouse. In 1823 the latter was moved to a new building up on the hill above St. Nicholas' Church on the site of what is now Dyke Road, where it remained till the original portion of the present building was erected at the top of Elm Grove in 1867. The dwelling of the monks, or the Prior's Lodge as it was called, which was just to the north of the Chapel, was acquired by the Town in 1584 for £44 and became the residence of the post-Reformation Vicars of Brighthelmston. In 1790 it was pulled down by the Rev. Thomas Hudson, who was Vicar from 1789 to 1804, and a new Vicarage erected a few yards to the north in Nile Street. This served as such until 1835, when the Rev. H. M. Wagner, who was Vicar from 1824 to 1870, employed Messrs. George Cheesman and Son to erect the new Vicarage at the top of Montpelier Road, which is now occupied by the Junior School of the Brighton and Hove High School for Girls. The building of 1790 was demolished in 1837. On some of the land surrounding the original Chantry or Grange, a market house was built in 1774. This was on the site of the present Town Hall. The town had been granted the right to hold a market by a charter of Edward II in 1313, and, until the end of the seventeenth or beginning of the eighteenth century, this had been held in a building beneath the cliff which was eventually overwhelmed by the sea. The existence of the medieval chapel of St. Bartholomews is still commemorated by the modern street name Bartholomews, and it is even possible that a fragment of an old wall, incorporated in the back of premises known as 44 Market Street, is part of the medieval building.

The Parish Church of Brighthelmston (Plate 2), dedicated to St. Nicholas, the patron saint of mariners and travellers, was built outside the original rectangle of the town on a hill to the north-west, as in the case of the contemporary Parish Church of Newhaven, then called Meeching before the estuary of the Ouse had abandoned Seaford in its favour. This was no doubt for safety both from the inroads of the sea and from raids by the French. The Domesday survey recorded that there was a church at Brighthelmston in 1081. But no portion of that structure remains, and it is not even certain whether it was on the same site or in the Lower Town beneath the cliff. The present building was erected about the middle of the fourteenth century. But little old work is visible in it to-day, as it was very much over-restored by R. C. Carpenter in 1853. Only the pillars and arches of the nave, the chancel arch and screen, and the tower survived this restoration. The chancel screen dates from the late fifteenth century. The clerestory was added by Somers Clarke in 1890. The chief glory of the church is its circular Norman stone font sculptured in four panels representing the Baptism of Christ, the Last Supper, and two scenes from the life of St. Nicholas. This survives from the older church and possibly came from the Priory of St. Pancras at Lewes. In 1743 the churchwardens of the day, to commemorate their zeal in having the font cleaned, caused their names to be carved upon its base. This so much horrified the Victorian restorers that they had the base of the font removed altogether. St. Nicholas's Church contains several memorials of interest. At the north-west corner of the nave is a large monument in fourteenth century style to the Duke of Wellington who as a boy worshipped in the Church when a pupil of the Rev. Henry Michell, Vicar from 1750 to 1789. This monument, designed by

R. C. Carpenter, was erected in 1853 by public subscription at the cost of £5,000 at the instigation of Henry Michell's grandson, the Rev. H. M. Wagner, a later Vicar. Another interesting memorial is that designed by the sculptor, Sir Richard Westmacott, in memory of his wife, who died at Brighton in 1834 and was buried in the Church. A tablet, erected in 1909 in the splay of one of the windows, records Dr. Johnson's association with Brighton, further mentioned in Chapter 2. Another tablet in the north-west corner of the church, near the Duke of Wellington's memorial, commemorates Thomas Read Kemp, the founder of Kemp Town. He died in Paris in 1844 and is buried in the cemetery of Père La Chaise. St. Nicholas's ceased to be the Parish Church of Brighton in 1873.

That the precaution of building the church upon a hill was not unnecessary was proved in 1514 when the French under their Admiral Prégent de Bidoux, variously called by the chroniclers of the time, 'Primauget', 'Prior Jehan' or 'Prior John', burned the town. The beacons on the Downs were lighted to summon the local levies to arms, and the French were eventually driven back to their ships by the English archers, but not before they had set fire to the town. Another similar raid may have occurred in 1545, but this is now considered doubtful. A contemporary drawing in the British Museum collection depicts the attack by the French in 1514 in actual progress, with the town in flames in the background.

As a result of the sack of the town by the French in 1514, no medieval buildings, other than St. Nicholas's Church, exist in Brighton to-day. But something of the character and pattern of the streets of those days survives in the Lanes (Plate 4). Though the buildings in these narrow passage-ways have been rebuilt and do not for the most part date from before the eighteenth century or even later, they still give a good idea of the form of streets in a medieval town, which were built in such a fashion that it was possible for people leaning out of upstairs windows on opposite sides of the street to shake hands across the street. Such a lay-out, though familiar enough to us in many continental towns and villages, is a rare enough survival in England to give the Lanes of Brighton a special claim on our attention. Even though they may contain few architectural features of note, they should certainly be preserved as walking thoroughfares which even to-day make a special contribution to the attractiveness of Brighton.

In the middle of the seventeenth century Brighthelmston springs for a brief moment into the limelight with the escape of Charles II. After the Battle of Worcester had been fought and lost on the 3rd September, 1651, Charles fled in disguise. After various adventures he made his way south as far as Heale, near Salisbury, where his only companion, Lord Wilmot, left him and went on into the north-west corner of Sussex to seek the assistance of Colonel Charles Gounter of Racton. A cottage at Racton, to this day called King Charles' Cottage, is still shown as a place where the King was concealed, but it seems to be very doubtful whether in fact he ever was hidden there. Lord Wilmot and Colonel Gounter made sundry attempts to charter a boat from one of the villages on or near Chichester Harbour, but without success. Their next move was to enter into negotiations with a merchant named Francis Mansell or Mancell who may have occupied Ovingdean Grange near Brighthelmston. After several unsuccessful attempts Mansell eventually discovered a seaman at Brighthelmston who agreed to make the passage. On 12th October, Colonel Gounter returned to fetch the King. They spent one night at Hambledon in Hampshire and on the 14th rode into Brighthelmston after passing without mishap through a troop of soldiers at Bramber. Harrison Ainsworth in his novel *Ovingdean Grange* writes of Charles spending a night at Mansell's house. But even if Francis Mansell did live at Ovingdean Grange, Charles certainly did not stay at or even visit the house. The association of his name with the Grange is entirely a figment of Ainsworth's imagination. The party put up at the George Inn at Brighthelmston, which, after the Restoration, naturally changed its name to the King's Head. There is considerable doubt as to the exact position of this inn. It was originally thought to be in West Street, but possibly it was another inn of the same name situated in Middle Street. While at the George, Charles was recognised by the innkeeper who had served in Charles I's bodyguard, but his secret was not betrayed. Francis Mansell then introduced Nicholas Tattersell, the Captain of the boat, *The Surprise*, which was to convey Charles to France. Tattersell drove a hard bargain and must clearly have recognised the identity of the distinguished refugee. He demanded and received no less than £200, which would be equivalent to at least £800 in modern currency. The next day, 15th October, 1651, the royal party set out from the inn at 2 a.m. to board Tattersell's boat, which was lying in a creek at Shoreham. Charles and Lord Wilmot said good-bye to Colonel Gounter, who returned home to his family, and the *Escape* set sail for France at 8 a.m. They landed safely at Fécamp in Normandy the same day. At the Restoration, Tattersell not unnaturally came forward to bask in the royal sunshine. He and his descendants were awarded a pension of £100 a year. His boat, re-named *The Royal Escape*, was taken into the King's nominal service as a fifth-rate ship of the Navy, and the pay of a Captain of such a craft accrued to its owner. Nicholas Tattersell became High Constable of Brighthelmston in 1670. He was not, it seems, a pleasant individual. He not only drove a hard bargain and afterwards posed as a loyalist of disinterested motives, but when in favour and office proved himself a vigorous persecutor of Dissenters

THE OLD TOWN

2 ST. NICHOLAS'S CHURCH, the old Parish Church of Brighton

3 COWLEY'S BUNN SHOPPE, POOL VALLEY

4 MEETING HOUSE LANE

5 OLD STEINE AND THE CHAIN PIER, during the 'Birthday' storm of the 24th November, 1824. *From a print by J. Bruce*

who, with the return of the King, found themselves harried by penal legislation, as had the Royalists in the days of the Puritans' power. Tattersell died in 1674 and is buried in St. Nicholas Churchyard just south of the Church, between the south wall of the building and the pathway.

CHAPTER TWO

Dr. Russell: Brighthelmston as a Spa

AT THE BEGINNING of the eighteenth century, particularly after the great storms of 1703 and 1705, the fortunes of Brighthelmston had sunk so low that in order to build wooden breakwaters to prevent further incursions by the sea resort was had to the charitable expedient of 'briefs', or offertories as they would now be called, whereby appeals, sanctioned by the Government, were made for such worthy local causes throughout the churches of the kingdom. From this state of decrepitude the town was only rescued in 1750 by the arrival of the real founder of modern Brighton, Dr. Richard Russell. Very little is known about the life of Dr. Russell, but his portrait by Zoffany can be seen in the Brighton Art Gallery (Plate 7). He came of a Lewes family and was born in the Parish of St. Michael, Lewes, in 1687. His father, Nathaniel Russell, was a surgeon and apothecary in that town at a period when these two callings were more or less identical and neither had a status much above the position of a tradesman. Richard Russell was educated at the Free Grammar School of St. Anne's, Lewes, and in due course became assistant to his father. He made a clandestine marriage with the only daughter of William Kempe of South Malling, Lewes, from which circumstance and from the fact that William Kempe occupied that very fine Queen Anne house, Malling Deanery, Lewes, one would presume that Russell's bride was considerably above his own station in life at the time. His wife's father was eventually reconciled to the match, and in due course Russell inherited and occupied Malling Deanery. After his marriage he went to the University of Leyden to study medicine. On his return he appears to have resided in London, was elected a Fellow of the Royal Society and became one of the Physicians of St. Thomas's Hospital. He subsequently moved back to Lewes, probably after his father's or his father-in-law's death, and practised there. He published several medical books, of which the most important was a Latin treatise entitled *De Tabe Glandulari*, which appeared in 1750. A translation of it, under the title 'A Dissertation Concerning the Use of Sea Water in Diseases of the Glands', was published in 1753. The publication of this work was one of the first occasions upon which any attention was directed to the usefulness or attractiveness of the sea in England and was thus not only the foundation of the future of Brighton, but in fact of the whole English sea-side. In addition to his recommendation of sea-water, Dr. Russell discovered the Chalybeate spring in what is now St. Ann's Well Gardens, Hove. He caused this to be enclosed within a basin and made use of it for treating patients whom he recommended to visit Brighthelmston. By 1754, these are said to have become so numerous that he built himself a permanent residence in the town in order to be able to supervise their treatment personally. Russell House occupied the site of the Royal Albion Hotel, Old Steine, and was, when built, the largest house in the town. Its garden on the south extended right down to the beach, though a wall was subsequently erected to protect it from the sea. Dr. Russell did not survive long enough to see the full effects of his discovery and patronage of Brighthelmston. He died in London on the 19th December, 1759, and was buried in the Kempe family vault at South Malling Church, Lewes. His only memorial is a small tablet on the east wall of the chancel and his burial in the church seems to be almost entirely forgotten to-day. It is not even mentioned in Frederick Harrison's *Notes on Sussex Churches*. Dr. Russell's eldest son, William, inherited Malling Deanery and assumed his mother's maiden name of Kempe. Russell House, Brighthelmston, remained a private house until 1807 and was occupied by George III's brother, the Duke of Cumberland, on several occasions. But it was subsequently divided into tenements and used for commercial or amusement purposes. Having become very dilapidated, it was pulled down in 1826 to make room for the Royal Albion Hotel. A tablet on the latter records Dr. Russell's connection with the spot.

During Dr. Russell's own lifetime his chief accomplishment might perhaps have been considered to be the fact that he was the first person to draw attention to the healing properties of sea water in any connection whatever. But to-day we are apt to consider it even more remarkable that he recommended his patients to drink, as well as to bathe in, sea water. He even went so far as to say that those who hurried into a course of bathing 'before the body is altered and sufficiently prepared by drinking sea water', thereby protracted their cure. To meet this requirement an ingenious gentleman named T. Swaine in 1756 resorted to the expedient of bottling sea water and advertising it in a London newspaper as for sale at the Talbot Inn, Southwark. Dr. Russell's successors, Dr. Relhan and Dr. Awsiter, varied the treatment by suggesting that the water might be taken hot or even mixed with milk, though Dr. Awsiter admitted that 'there are many constitutions too delicate, and stomachs too weak, to bear the nausea and sickness it' (the drinking of sea water) 'produces, and even where this inconvenience is overcome by struggles, it makes the party very thirsty for the remainder of the day'.

Even bathing was not intended to give pleasure to the persons indulging in it and no doubt did not do so when one recollects that it was not uncommon for people to bathe by moonlight before dawn on a November morning. The process involved entering a machine built on high wooden wheels and drawn by a horse. When the visitor had undressed and donned the loose robe in which the plunge was to be made, the machine was drawn into the sea and the horse's head turned back towards the shore. On the steps of the machine stood an official 'bather', as the men attendants were called, or 'dipper' in the case of the women, who seized the 'bathee' in his or her arms and plunged him or her several times vigorously in the water, no doubt without any regard to whether the water entered his or her eyes, nose and mouth. Very few people at this period knew how to swim and were willing to enter the water unattended. Those who did so were looked upon with extreme disfavour by the 'bathers' for dispensing with their services and by the other visitors for monopolising for so long a period one of the machines, of which the sum total in the whole town was at first only 12. The sexes were of course strictly segregated when bathing. The ladies' bathing place was just east of Russell House, the gentlemen's further west. It became a favourite pastime for the gentlemen on shore to watch through telescopes and spy glasses the ladies emerge from and re-enter the machines, particularly if the wind, of which there has never been any lack in Brighton, was likely to assist them by revealing rather more than usual of what they hoped to see. Rowlandson has most vividly depicted for us a group of sightseers engaged in this gleeful occupation.

The bathers and dippers of Brighthelmston occupied a very important place in the town's history. The most celebrated of the men was John, or Smoaker, Miles, who in due course was succeeded by his brother William, sometimes called Smoaker II. Smoaker was the possessor of a ready wit and is the subject of several anecdotes exemplifying this. The best perhaps relates to two dandies who once accosted him with the remark that they had come down to Brighton for the benefit of their health and had been recommended to drink asses' milk. They proceeded to enquire whether he could inform them where this could be obtained; to which Smoaker unhesitatingly replied that they could not do better than suck each other. Even to the Prince of Wales, Smoaker did not hesitate to speak his mind in his own bluff and genial manner. On one occasion the Prince expressed his intention of bathing when Smoaker thought it too rough to be safe and persisted despite these objections. Smoaker stepped in front of him and putting himself in a boxing attitude exclaimed: 'Come! come! this won't do; I'll be damned if you shall bathe. What do you think your father would say to me if you were drowned? He would say, this is all owing to you, Smoaker! If you had taken proper care of him, poor George would have still been alive.' The Prince thereupon desisted. On another occasion when the Prince swam out further than Smoaker thought prudent and proceeded to ignore his cries of 'Mr. Prince, Mr. Prince, come back', Smoaker went so far as to swim out to him, seize him by the ear and pull him back to the shore. When the Prince remonstrated with him, he remarked 'I ar'nt agoen' to let the King hang me for letten' the Prince of Wales drown hisself; not I, to please nobody, I can tell 'e'. Smoaker was in fact devoted to the Prince of Wales and once walked all the way to London to enquire after his health. Smoaker Miles died in 1794 and was buried in St. Nicholas's Churchyard near the west wall opposite Upper North Street, but the tombstone had become indecipherable and therefore unidentifiable as far back as 1862.

Smoaker Miles's daughter, Abigail, was one of the dippers. This term derived from an inland watering place where women were employed to dip glasses in the wells and hand them to the visitors. Two of the original dippers were Mary Cobby and Mary Howell. But the 'Queen of 'em all', as she was called by a local song, was the celebrated Martha Gunn. Her family was one that had been established in Brighthelmston for at least 200 years and exists even to-day. One of the few premises which have retained their early nineteenth century shop fronts intact, No. 102 St. James's Street, is still occupied by a member of this family, and their connection with the sea survives also, as the shop is a fishmonger's. Martha Gunn was born in 1726 and carried on the profession of dipper from the very institution of official bathing in 1750. She was the acknowledged 'Queen of the Bath', and Smoaker's daughter was said to be only her handmaiden. Her reign lasted so long that she became a celebrity known to the whole of society, since, long before she died, Brighthelmston had become the most fashionable provincial town in the Kingdom. Eventually infirmity and increasing stoutness forced her to give up actually bathing ladies, but she continued until her death to superintend on the beach. She died on the 2nd May, 1815, aged 89 and was buried in St. Nicholas's Churchyard, where her tombstone can still be seen just south-east of the porch. Her portrait in pastels by J. Russell, R.A., now hangs in Buckingham Palace beside that of Smoaker Miles by the same artist, and shows her round knobbly countenance enveloped in an immense hat the shape of an inverted coal-scuttle. She was the prototype of many another such figure amongst the womenkind of the sea-faring folk of Brighton. Even in our own day two well-known figures greatly resembling her in general appearance can be seen daily in Castle Square, one selling flowers and the other newspapers, and the flower-seller is actually a member of the Gunn family.

Another local celebrity who was a contemporary of Martha Gunn and who is buried only a few yards to the

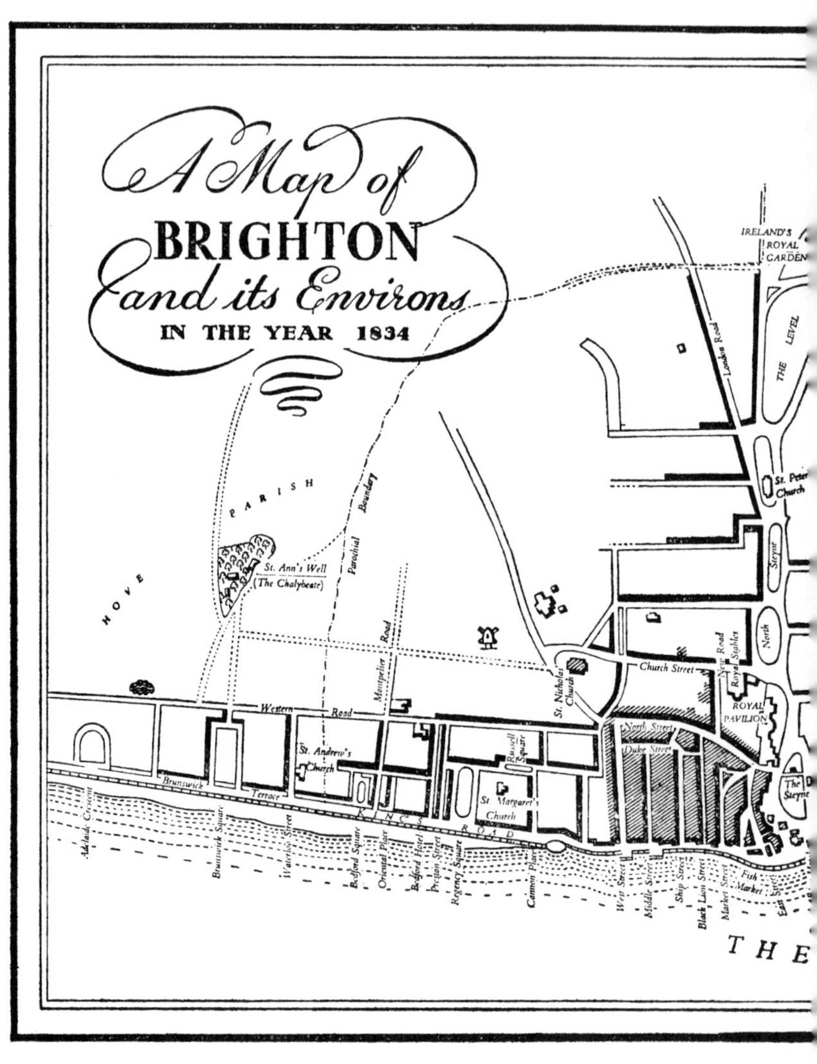

This adaptation of Saunder's map of 1834 demonstrates the rapid growth

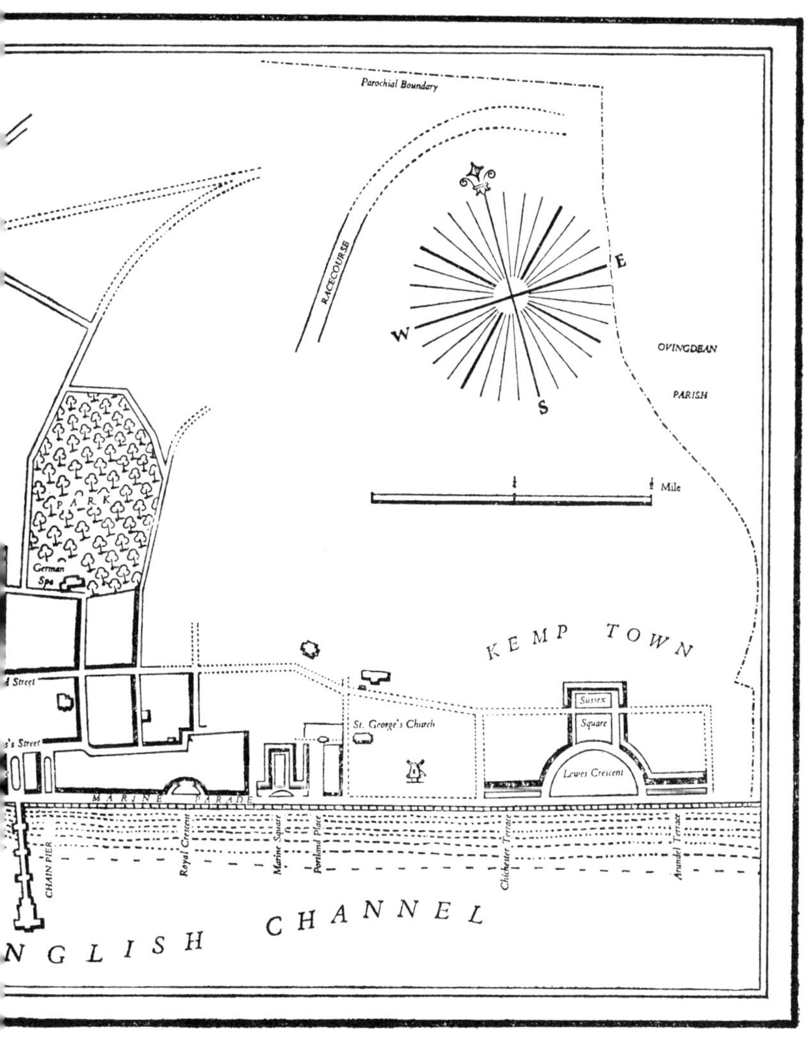

of Brighton. The shaded portion shows the extent of the Town in 1779.

east of her tomb in St. Nicholas's Churchyard, was Phoebe Hessel who had a most adventurous career, though not in connection with the sea. She was born in 1713 and when but 15 years of age fell in love with a private soldier named Golding in the regiment known as Kirke's Lambs. His regiment being ordered to the West Indies, she disguised herself as a man and enlisted in the 5th Regiment of Foot, which was posted to the same station. She served in the Army for at least 17 years without her sex ever being discovered and was even wounded in the arm at the Battle of Fontenoy. When Golding was later wounded at Gibraltar and invalided home, she confessed her story to the wife of the General in Command of her Regiment and obtained her discharge. She and Golding were then married and lived happily together for more than 20 years. After his death she married a certain William Hassell or Hessel who lived in Brighthelmston. He died about 1792. Phoebe then purchased a donkey and hawked fish and other commodities in the neighbouring villages to the west. About 1800 she was obliged to give up this active occupation on account of advancing years and became dependent upon parish relief, supplemented by the sale of bulls-eyes, pin cushions and other small articles which she dispensed from a spot near the junction of Old Steine and Marine Parade. By the end of the Napoleonic wars she had become—at the age of 101—the oldest inhabitant of Brighthelmston, and as such sat on the left of the Vicar, the Rev. Robert Carr, at the festivities to celebrate the peace in 1814. At the coronation of George IV in 1820, Phoebe, then aged 107, was still alive, though quite blind, and was able to take part in the local celebrations in the same capacity. During the last few years of her life the Prince Regent allowed her a pension of half a guinea a week. It is said that he offered her a guinea a week but that she refused this, saying that half a guinea was sufficient for her needs. She died on the 12th December, 1821, aged 108.

CHAPTER THREE

Visitors: The Arrival of the Prince of Wales

IN SPITE of the unattractive nature of the prescriptions recommended by Dr. Russell and his successors, patients and visitors soon flocked to Brighthelmston in large numbers.

One of the first people of importance to visit the town was Selina, Countess of Huntingdon, who brought her youngest son to the sea-side to try a course of sea bathing for the benefit of his health. In 1755 the Countess took a house in North Street and from then on resided there frequently. Her child died in 1757, but she returned to Brighthelmston a few years later. On this occasion, in 1760, George Whitefield, who was her Chaplain, preached several times in a field behind the White Lion Inn, North Street. A small band of fellow worshippers came together as the result of these sermons, and it became necessary to provide them with a meeting place. The Countess would gladly have given the money for this, but her extensive charitable gifts had for the time being exhausted her funds. To meet the need she sold her jewels. They raised £698 15s. 0d., and with these proceeds a small chapel was built in 1761 behind the Countess's house in North Street. This chapel was the original Countess of Huntingdon's Church which still occupies the same site to-day. It has been enlarged and rebuilt several times. The present building dates from 1870. The chapel was incidentally not the first dissenting meeting place to be established in Brighthelmston. The earliest, dated 1683, was on the site of the present

Tabernacle of the Elim Four Square Gospel, Union Street, in the Lanes. The date-stone of the original chapel can still be seen in the south wall of this building, though it was entirely rebuilt by Amon Wilds in 1825. The Countess of Huntingdon's Chapel was also preceded by the Friend's Meeting House, built in 1700-1701, which stood almost opposite to it in North Street. This was demolished in 1800, and the Meeting House transferred to the present building in Ship Street, which was altered and enlarged in 1876.

Amongst other early visitors to Brighthelmston were Henry and Hester Thrale, the friends of Dr. Johnson. Their introduction to the town is said to have been one of necessity rather than choice. In 1771-2 Henry Thrale suffered serious losses in his business and was reduced to considerable straits for money. In this need he had resort to an old friend of his father's named Richard Scrase, a solicitor of fortune who had practised for many years in Seaford but who, in 1771, had retired to Brighthelmston. Mrs. Thrale came down to Brighthelmston to seek the old man's assistance and was successful in obtaining a loan of £6,000 from him—a very large sum for those days. Whether it was that on this visit Mrs. Thrale took a fancy to the town, or whether the old gentleman desired frequent reports as to the safety of his money, one cannot say. But as a result of this visit the Thrales acquired a permanent establishment in Brighthelmston. They were one of the first families to build themselves a house in the town for their annual visits. This was a low stone coloured brick building which stood at the south end of the east side of West Street, opposite the King's Head Inn. It was demolished in 1866 to make room for the Grand Concert Hall which was itself destroyed by fire in 1882. Sherry's Dance Hall now stands on the site.

Hither the Thrales came almost every year until Henry Thrale's death in 1781. One of their children, a son named

Ralph, who was born in 1773, died at their house in Brighthelmston on the 17th July, 1775, and was buried in St. Nicholas's Church. Fanny Burney was frequently with them, and Dr. Johnson visited them there more than once. The ladies were great enthusiasts for sea bathing and either by the force of example or persuasion induced Dr. Johnson to venture into the sea. One of the 'bathers', on seeing Johnson in the water, is said to have remarked: 'Why, Sir, you must have been a stout-hearted gentleman 40 years ago.'

Bathing was not the only unaccustomed occupation in which Johnson indulged while at Brighthelmston. He also rode to hounds. Though he covered 50 miles in the day, he did not find the experience exhilarating, and his comment on the pursuit was little less scathing than Oscar Wilde's. But he was no more immune than most eminent persons from that strange lack of proportion which often lends them to prefer to their special distinction in their own sphere, some quite trifling accomplishment that men with only a particle of their capacities could achieve far better than they. He was in this instance childishly delighted at hearing Single-Speech Hamilton exclaim: 'Why, Johnson rides as well, for aught I see, as the most illiterate fellow in England.' It was no doubt the view of the countryside that he obtained from the Downs when out with the hounds that inspired his famous growl about Brighthelmston, that it was 'so truly desolate that if one had a mind to hang oneself for desperation on being obliged to live there, it would be difficult to find a tree on which to fasten the rope'. With the conversation within doors he was not much better satisfied and during a ball which the Thrales attended he engaged in a violent dispute with the Vicar, the Rev. Henry Michell, in which, after each party had failed to subdue the other by shouting, Michell took up the poker and Johnson the tongs, and both endeavoured to drive home their points by thumping on the grate with these implements until, amidst the alarm of the dancers, they were pacified and separated by the intervention of the Master of Ceremonies.

The fourth Duke of Marlborough became a regular visitor of Brighton from 1767 onwards, but it will be more convenient to describe his house in the Chapter 4 relating to the Steine.

In July,1765, Royalty made its first appearance in the town in the person of the Duke of Gloucester, younger brother of George III, who the following year married Horace Walpole's niece, Maria, Countess of Waldegrave. All George III's brothers, with whom he was on bad terms, chiefly on account of their morganatic marriages, came to Brighthelmston at this period. The Duke of York paid a brief visit in 1766, and the Duke of Cumberland followed in 1771. The last is the most important of the three in the chronicles of Brighthelmston, since he was so well pleased with his stay that he returned in the following year; and again in 1779 after his marriage. In fact he rented a house in Brighthelmston every season for the next four or five years and built up quite a little court around himself there. His relations with the King were perhaps worse than those of his other two brothers because his wife, Anne Horton, in addition to her lack of royal birth, combined with this a complete absence of reputation, which made her in George III's eyes an even more unwelcome sister-in-law than the Duchess of Gloucester. In the Duke and Duchess of Cumberland's circle life was fast and the company far from select. It was natural, therefore, that the Prince of Wales who, as he approached his majority, was just about to embark upon that process of lifelong struggle and opposition between the occupant of the throne and the heir apparent, which was almost hereditary in the House of Hanover, should be attracted to his uncle's circle. This offered him everything that he had lacked at

Windsor: freedom, gaiety, amusement and entertaining company. The Prince of Wales came of age on August 12th, 1783, and on the 7th September paid his first visit to Brighthelmston amidst the acclamations of a large part of the population assembled to greet him at the entrance to the town (Plate 8). In addition to the motive already mentioned, it is likely that the Prince came to the seaside for the purpose of sea bathing, which was then held to be an effective remedy for swellings in the glands of his neck—presumably goitre—from which he then suffered, and to conceal which he was in the habit all his life of wearing a high stock. The Prince remained eleven days with the Duke of Cumberland at Grove House which occupied the site of the north-east corner of the Royal Pavilion. He enjoyed himself so much that he returned in July the following year and occupied the same house. Further visits succeeded in 1785 and 1786, and in fact these became an annual occurrence thenceforward. But their history after 1786 belongs to the story of the Royal Pavilion related in Chapter 6.

The arrival of George IV—to give him his eventual title—was probably the most important event in the whole history of Brighton, for, if not the founder of the town—a role which belonged to Dr. Russell—he occupied a unique position in its history. Sir Osbert Sitwell and Miss Margaret Barton have called him the 'Patron Saint of Brighton'. This seems not quite the right term. 'Saint' is hardly an appropriate word to apply to George IV, although it is true that his portrait by Sir Thomas Lawrence, which had been sent as a gift to Pope Pius VII, was once placed over the altar of a church and treated with the veneration implied by such a position. During cleaning operations at the Vatican it was confused with other pictures and by mistake sent to the Church of St. John Lateran. There it was taken for the picture of a saint and used as an altar piece until the mistake was pointed out by the English artists Joseph Severn and George Richmond who were then living in Rome. Patron, however, is abundantly right, for if he did not found Brighton, he made it a resort of world-wide renown. Brighton is bound, therefore, to take a lenient view of George IV. Elsewhere he is perhaps looked upon as one of the least reputable occupants of the English throne. But if his failings were considerable, we should be grateful to him for two developments of which the benefit is still felt even to-day. Together with his friend, Brummell, he was largely responsible for making personal cleanliness an accepted fashion in polite circles—a welcome change from the filth of the seventeenth century which had lingered on well into the eighteenth. Secondly, he was one of the first people to insist that shoes were made with a right and left foot and not left for the wearer to make these for himself. These achievements are perhaps even more important to the community than the fact that he was a lavish patron of the arts and greatly enriched the royal collection of pictures, which are sometimes held to be his chief claim upon the gratitude of posterity. In Brighton in any case his worst defects were always less in evidence; his good points were most emphasised. His generosity to local causes made up for his extravagance. His friendliness and good humour were more noticeable than his inconstancy. His good taste in art and architecture outweighed his bad taste in youthful friends. The pleasure resort into which his patronage transformed the spa of 1750 has lived up to its name in no small measure in the one hundred and fifty years since his day and has given pleasure literally to millions. For this he is entitled to the gratitude of those whom he has benefited. In the construction of the Pavilion—that unique building—he also acquired for himself a special claim to indulgent consideration at our hands; but this will be mentioned more fully in Chapter 6.

6 OLD STEINE AND THE ROYAL PAVILION, AFTER 1834. *From a print by J. Bruce*

FOUNDER AND PATRON

7 DR. RICHARD RUSSELL by ZOFFANY. (*Reproduced by kind permission of Brighton Art Gallery and Museum*)

8 GEORGE, PRINCE OF WALES by HOPPNER. (*Reproduced by kind permission of Lord Sherwood*)

CHAPTER FOUR

The Steine

FOR AT LEAST 20 or 30 years after Brighthelmston was discovered by Dr. Russell the accommodation for visitors remained extremely inadequate. In fact such lodging houses as were available were only two-storied fishermen's cottages, fronted with tarred cobbles or knapped flints. They were usually entered by a step down from the street level and often had such low ceilings that tall people were unable to stand upright in some of the rooms. Few of these little houses survive to-day, but a good example can be seen at 12 Brighton Place. The old town at Hastings gives us some idea of the nature of Brighthelmston of that day. A few houses of more spacious proportions were, however, built in the centre of the town during the last half of the century, such as Nos. 10 and 15 Prince Albert Street. The ground floor of No. 10, including the doorway, is a modern reconstruction and an excellent example of how well the restoration of a Georgian building can be carried out.

The only two hotels of consequence were the Old Ship and the Castle. Although the former, as an inn, dates back further than any other licensed house in Brighton, none of its present building is old, except the Assembly Rooms behind, which were built in 1767. These comprise a Ballroom with a gallery for the musicians and a Card-room adjoining. The Castle Hotel stood on the site of the modern Electricity Showrooms at the north-east corner of Castle Square. It was opened in 1755. A Ballroom, designed by John Crunden was added in 1766. In 1822 the whole building was purchased by George IV, and the Ballroom converted into the Royal Chapel. The rest of the hotel was pulled down in the following year. An L-shaped stuccoed terrace was then built on the south-east corner of the site. This terrace in its turn was demolished in 1930 to make room for the Electricity Showrooms. When the Royal Pavilion was purchased by Brighton Corporation in 1850, the Chapel was claimed by the Ecclesiastical Authorities, demolished and re-erected as St. Stephen's Church in Montpelier Place, where it still stands, though it has been closed since 1939 (Plate 22).

When the town began to spread beyond the rectangle of the old fishing village, its first expansion was to the east. On this site was a piece of rough grass or common land chiefly used by the fishermen for drying their nets. Its name of the Steine derives from a Scandinavian or Flemish word meaning a stone, no doubt of ancient ceremonial origin. Through the Steine ran a stream called the Wellsbourn, which had its source at Patcham and reached the Steine *via* the Pool or Valley to the north. This is no doubt the stream to which antiquaries refer when they allege that the name of Brighthelmston derives from 'brist' or 'briz', betokening division. The stream still exists but now flows underground to the sea.

The earliest house facing the Steine was the old Manor House—a small two-storied red brick building on the south side with its back to the sea. It was occupied from 1771-1792 by Richard Scrase, the friend of the Thrales, and one of the joint Lords of the Manor of Brighthelmston. After his death it was enlarged and continued to exist until 1817, when the Royal York Hotel, now Royal York Buildings, was built on the site.

To the east was Russell House, erected in 1754 and demolished in 1826 to make way for the Royal Albion Hotel.

After the latter, the next house both in importance and date to be erected was Marlborough House. This was built in 1769 by Samuel Shergold, the proprietor of the Castle Hotel. Two years later it was sold to the fourth Duke of Marlborough. He retained the house until 1786, when it was purchased by William Gerald Hamilton, M.P., or Single-Speech Hamilton as he is better known. Hamilton employed Robert Adam to rebuild the house, and under Adam's direction it assumed its present form. The Prince of Wales, with his bride, Caroline of Brunswick, stayed there in 1795. Hamilton died in 1796, and from 1801 until 1818 the house was occupied by Lady Anne Murray, sister of Lord Mansfield. Marlborough House, which has retained its original name, is architecturally the most distinguished individual house still standing in the town (Plate 9). It is now used as the Education Offices of Brighton Corporation. But all the rooms except the Board Room having been divided by partitions, its fine interior cannot be seen to advantage. When the new Town Hall is built, it is to be hoped that this will be remedied. The house would make a splendid centre for the cultural activities of the town.

When the Duke of Marlborough gave up his original residence in Brighthelmston, he first rented and then, in 1790, purchased from Percy Wyndham, brother of the Earl of Egremont, another house further north on the Steine. This was a large red brick farm house named Grove House, erected prior to 1779. It had been rented by the Duke of Cumberland in 1783 when he had entertained the Prince of Wales on his first visit to Brighthelmston and was again occupied by the Prince in 1784. When purchased by the Duke it was re-named Marlborough House. This duplication of the name in connection with a second house on the Steine has led to a certain amount of confusion. The house stood on the site of the present Music Room of the Royal Pavilion. It was purchased by the Prince Regent in 1812 and demolished to enlarge the Pavilion.

To the south of this second Marlborough House stood another farm house of moderate size which belonged to Thomas Kemp, one of the Joint Lords of the Manor of Brighthelmston. This was leased on behalf of the Prince of Wales in 1786 and purchased outright a year later. From it emerged the Royal Pavilion, of which the history is given in Chapter 6.

The last important individual house on the Steine that need be mentioned is Steine House, immediately to the north of the first Marlborough House. But as this was not built until 1801 and replaced an older building, its history belongs to a later chapter.

The first building on the east side of the Steine was Baker's Library, which stood at the south-west corner of what is now St. James's Street. Donowell's print of 1778 shows this standing in complete isolation. But soon after 1780 a series of houses was built to the north and south of it, forming the east side of the Steine. These two blocks, separated by St. James's Street, were at first known as North and South Parade, recalling the fashionable terraces of that name at Bath. At the north end of North Parade were four houses at right angles to it (Plate 6). On the occasion of one of the Prince of Wales' visits to the town these were painted with the Whig colours of blue and buff and were ever afterwards known as 'the Blues and Buffs'. Two of these four houses (Nos. 1 and 2 Old Steine) have unfortunately been the victims of road-widening, but Nos. 3 and 4 remain. Almost all the houses in the Steine that were built at this period have been re-fronted since, either in George IV's reign or later, particularly those of South Parade, between St. James's Street and the sea, which to-day have little unity of design. The three southernmost houses of North Parade have been demolished, but almost all the others in this section of the Steine have retained their original doorways, even though the rest of

9 MARLBOROUGH HOUSE, OLD STEINE

10 ROYAL CRESCENT

11 A CONCERT AT TUPPEN AND WALKER'S ROYAL MARINE LIBRARY. *From a print after C. W. Wing*

12 IRELAND'S ROYAL BRIGHTON GARDENS. *From a print by R. Sickelmore*

13 MAHOMED'S BATHS. *From a print after J. Cordwell*

the fronts have been re-faced. Almost the only houses that retain the whole of their original façades unaltered are No. 3 in the 'Blues and Buffs', No. 12 on the east side, and Nos 44—46 on the south side adjoining Royal York Buildings. No. 3 in particular is a good example of a small house in vernacular style fronted with cobbles set off by painted brick window surrounds and quoins. Princes Street, the continuation to the north of the east side of the Steine, was also built at this time and likewise retains a few of its elegant contemporary doorways. Pavilion Parade in front of it with its two excellent houses at the north end, fronted with tarred cobbles and with painted brick window surrounds and quoins, followed about 1800.

The Steine at first presented a rather rough and ready appearance. It was unenclosed. Fishermen spread out their nets to dry and hauled up their boats there during storms. Little black pigs wandered around scavenging. From time to time the Wellsbourn flooded the whole area. Gradually it was made more attractive. The first step was to level and enclose it partially with common hurdles. In 1793 the Wellsbourn was encased in an arched brick sewer* and the Pool to the north filled up. Then wooden railings were erected all round the grass, and in 1806 the circumference immediately within the railings was paved with bricks to form a path all round. The wooden palings were replaced by iron railings in 1822-3, despite the objections of the fishermen who lost the right to dry their nets on the Steine when this complete enclosure took place. These railings were only removed in our own time. There was a footpath across the centre from Castle Square to St. James's Street, but no roadway. Wheeled traffic proceeding from Castle Square to the Blues and Buffs had to go south along the west side of the Steine into Pool Valley, round the

* The Wellsbourn still flowed in this brick channel until 1875, when the construction of the Waterworks at Patcham diverted the supply of water.

back of the York Hotel into the Steine again in front of Russell House, along the east side of the Steine as far as the island site of Thomas's Library at the bottom of St. James's Street, behind this into St. James's Street itself and thence along the remainder of the east side of the Steine. The carriage road along the south of the Steine in front of the York Hotel was opened in 1826, but it was not until 1834 that a road for wheeled traffic was opened from Castle Square to St. James's Street across the enclosure.

CHAPTER FIVE

Fashionable Life in Brighthelmston

ORIGINALLY the season at Brighthelmston was from June to September. Visitors were conveyed thither by coach from the Golden Cross Inn, Charing Cross. In 1792 the journey took normally nine hours, but more often eleven. The single fare was 14s. The journey was not, however, the romantic delight that Christmas cards suggest. Passengers were obliged to walk up all and down some of the hills. Out of the 32 miles between Reigate and Brighthelmston, it was calculated that the passengers walked 20. The coachmen insisted on stopping at every public house that they passed, both for their own refreshment and no doubt because they were well rewarded by the publicans for the trade which they brought. Every inn along the road had its own speciality to offer travellers. The Red Lion at Handcross provided gin and gingerbread, which the landlord himself dispensed outside the building from a gallon bottle and a wicker basket respectively. The inn at Staplefield was famous for the hostess's rabbit puddings and in season for black cherries locally grown. The terminus of the coaches in Brighthelmston was at first the Old Ship, the Castle, or other inns. Later passengers were set down at special coach offices. Visitors' first concern on arrival was to inscribe their names at one of the local Libraries. The two earliest Libraries were Woodgate's, later successively Widget's, Bowen's, Crawford's, Fisher's, and Shaw's, which was situated on the south side of the Steine near the old Manor House and the Post Office, and

Baker's, later successively Thomas's, Dudlow's, Gregory's, and Donaldson's, at the south-west corner of St. James's Street. The original building was demolished in 1806, when the premises were enlarged. Raggett's subscription house at the opposite corner of St. James's Street was a third establishment of this kind. A fourth, established in 1798 on Marine Parade, between Manchester Street and Charles Street, was run by Messrs. Donaldson & Wilkes, later by a Mr. Pollard, and subsequently by Messrs. Tuppen & Walker. These Libraries were very important institutions in the Brighthelmston of the day and in fact constituted the nearest approach to a pump-room that the town has ever had. Each had a colonnade or covered walk beneath which subscribers congregated to read the newspapers and watch the other members of the fashionable world disporting themselves on the Steine. Inside, regular entertainments were provided. These at first took the form of raffles. But raffling having subsequently been made illegal by an Act of Parliament known as 'Mr. Vansittart's Little-go Bill', trinket auctions were substituted. Loo, or Pam, and other card games were played assiduously, and later, when the rage for gambling which so characterised the end of the 18th century had somewhat abated, concert performances were given in their stead four times a day, at 2, 3, 5 and 8 o'clock, no doubt to provide that degree of inaudibility which is considered such an indispensible stimulus of conversation in fashionable resorts (Plate 11). But the main object of visitors in frequenting the Libraries was to study the list of new arrivals. The Master of Ceremonies maintained a book at each of these establishments in which all visitors inscribed their names, the list being subsequently published in the 'Fashionable Chronicle' of the local newspapers. At the same time they deposited a guinea which entitled them to call upon the good offices of the Master of Ceremonies for such matters as introductions, decisions in disputes as to precedence and the general regulation of all matters of etiquette and propriety.

The first Master of Ceremonies, Captain William Wade, was appointed in 1767 and reigned until his death in 1808. Until 1777 he also fulfilled the same function at Bath during the winter season. The second half of the eighteenth century was the hey-day of the Master of Ceremonies' ascendancy in Brighthelmston, and his influence was then unchallenged. His chief function comprised the supervision of the balls at the Old Ship and the Castle Assembly Rooms. Little is known about Captain Wade's personality. He was succeeded by William Forth, who lasted until 1828 but seems to have been an even more colourless person. The third and last of the dynasty was Lieutenant-Colonel John Eld. Sydney Smith has described him for us in a passage which has been often quoted but gives so vivid a picture of this social potentate that it will bear repetition. '*Who* he is, I know not; but I am certain *what* he is. It is that distinguished functionary the Master of Ceremonies. It could be no one else. It was a gentleman attired "*point device*", walking down the Parade, like Agag, "*delicately*". He pointed out his toes like a dancing-master; but carried his head like a potentate. As he passed the stand of flys, he nodded approval, as if he owned them all. As he approached the little goat carriages, he looked askance over the edge of his starched neckcloth and blandly smiled encouragement. Sure that in following him, I was treading in the steps of greatness, I went on to the Pier and there I was confirmed in my conviction of his eminence; for I observed him look first over the right side and then over the left, with an expression of serene satisfaction spreading over his countenance, which said, as plainly as if he had spoken to the sea aloud, "That is right. You are low tide at present; but never mind, in a couple of hours, I will make you high tide again".' By Colonel Eld's day the vast concourse of visitors who frequented the town and the modification of some of the strict formalities which characterised the social life of the eighteenth century had greatly altered the scope and degree of his authority. With the arrival of the railway in 1841, the office became almost obsolete, though Colonel Eld lingered on until as late as 1855.

In Captain Wade's day, the chief rival in the entertainment world to the balls at the Old Ship and the Castle, consisted of theatrical performances. These were first held in a barn on the west side of the Steine. But in 1774 the first permanent building was opened in North Street, opposite Windsor Street. This was used until 1789. In the following year the licence was transferred to another building in Duke Street. When the latter was demolished in 1807, the theatre was again moved, this time to the site of the present Theatre Royal in New Road. The original conveyance of the land signed by George IV is still in existence. The foundation stone was laid on the 10th September, 1806, and the first performance was given on the 27th June, 1807. The cost of the building, including the scenery, the wardrobe and a cottage adjoining the theatre which was occupied by the manager, amounted to £12,000. Here, almost every famous English actor and actress from Sarah Siddons to our own day has appeared upon the stage, though the actual building of the Theatre dates from later in the century. It was particularly celebrated at the end of the century under the management of Mrs. Nye Chart.

In the day-time racing was a very favourite diversion. The earliest recorded horse race at Brighthelmston took place on the Downs in 1770. It was not until 1783 that organised races as we know them to-day were instituted. Thenceforward they became an annual event patronised by the Prince of Wales, the Duke of Cumberland, the odious Duke of Orleans, and all other visitors of distinction.

During the Napoleonic Wars considerable quantities of troops were quartered in Brighthelmston, both in barracks in West Street and in special camps established on the outskirts of the town. The officers of the regiments quartered here who, it will be remembered, so occupied the imagination of Lydia Bennett in *Pride and Prejudice*, were amongst the most assiduous patrons of the races. These camps have left their permanent memorial behind them in the song 'The Girl I Left Behind Me', of which the sub-title is 'The Brighton Camp'. So great at this period was the passion for racing and the betting to which this gave rise, that impromptu races were sometimes organised on the Steine; for men encumbered with heavy weights, for country girls, for people in sacks, for donkeys and other animals, in short, for almost anything that could move. Sometimes these events were held in the Promenade Grove, a public garden established in 1793 and modelled on the Vauxhall Gardens, London. The Grove occupied the site of the Western Lawns of the Royal Pavilion between Church Street and Prince's Place. But the more usual festivities of this establishment were public breakfasts served in the open air, concerts, and displays of fireworks and illuminations. The life of the Promenade Grove ended in 1802, when it was purchased by the Prince of Wales and thrown into the Pavilion Grounds.

Cricket was a very popular game of the period. The ground used by the Prince of Wales and his friends was the north end of what is now called the Level. After the Prince gave up playing, Thomas Read Kemp, to whom the land belonged, made a grant of part of it to the Town Commissioners for use as a permanent open space. A portion of it at the north end was purchased by James Ireland, a local worthy who had an interesting and varied career. In 1806 he had purchased from Daniel and William Constable the draper's business which these two brothers had established at 3 North Street in 1802. Ireland carried on the business of a woollen draper and undertaker there and at No. 10 North Street until 1822, when he sold both premises to Mr. Hannington, the founder of the firm of that name, who also acquired the adjoining business of William Diplock at No. 4 North Street.

James Ireland proceeded to lay out the ten acres of land which he had purchased from Thomas Read Kemp as a pleasure ground or subscription garden which was intended to revive and surpass in splendour and variety the attractions of the Promenade Grove (Plate 12). There was a large cricket ground, for which the claim was made that it had the finest piece of turf in England; a ladies' bowling green surrounded by a lawn and ten arbours; a sheet of water spanned by a bridge; a building comprising reading, refreshment and dressing rooms and a 'promenade room' over; an aviary and grotto; a Gothic tower and gateway; and a maze, in the centre of which was a 'Merlin swing'—whatever that may have been. Displays of fireworks were given, and on one occasion a demonstration of 'flying' was arranged. A cable was stretched from the top of the tower to the foot of the bridge. A man was attached to this longitudinally and by an arrangement of wheels revolving round the cable, glided gracefully down, waving a flag in each hand.

In spite of all these attractions, the Royal Brighton Gardens, or Ireland's Gardens as they were more often called, proved a failure; James Ireland lost all the money he had invested in them. He was compelled to sell them and turned publican. In addition to the Hanover Arms adjoining the Gardens, he also ran the Golden Cross Inn in Prince's Street. He later moved to the Kerrison Arms at Hove and at the same time took up the office of Rate Collector to the Brunswick Square Commissioners, which he held till his death in 1842. The Gardens passed through several

14 HENRY HOLLAND'S PAVILION. (*Reproduced by permission of Brighton Art Gallery and Museum*)

15 THE ROYAL PAVILION, EAST FRONT

16 CONSOLE TABLE AND MIRROR, made for the Royal Pavilion. (*Reproduced by kind permission of Lord Sherwood*)

17 No. 1 EASTERN TERRACE, THE STAIRCASE

18 STEINE HOUSE, OLD STEINE, THE STAIRC

hands, gradually becoming more neglected, and after being used for a short time as a menagerie and fair ground, were broken up and Park Crescent built upon the site in 1829. The cricket matches played at Ireland's Gardens are commemorated by Mason's well-known print of a match between Sussex and Kent in 1842, though this actually took place on the Level after it had been severed from the site of the Gardens by the construction of Park Crescent.

CHAPTER SIX

The Royal Pavilion

ON THE OCCASION of the Prince of Wales' first visit to Brighthelmston in 1783, again in the following year and possibly in 1785, he occupied Grove House, later known as Marlborough House, at the north-west corner of the Steine. In 1786 Louis Weltje, the Clerk of the Prince's Kitchen, acting on the Prince's behalf, took a lease from Thomas Kemp of the adjoining house to the south. A year later Weltje purchased it outright.

The Prince immediately commissioned Henry Holland, who was then working for him at Carlton House in London, to build him a house on the site. This was erected with remarkable speed, as it was in occupation by July, 1787. The Marine Pavilion of His Royal Highness, as it was called, consisted of a letter E in plan, of which the main front faced east (Plate 14). This had in the centre a semi-circular portico of six Ionic columns surmounted by statues above the entablature, with a small recessed dome, and on each side of this central feature two slightly less curved bows with a delicate iron balcony on the first floor. The name of the Pavilion, which has clung to the building through all its later developments, was entirely appropriate to the simple classical character of Holland's building. The central room, known as the Saloon, which was the shape of an ellipse enlarged by a semi-circular recess to the north and south, was decorated by Biagio Rebecca who carried out so much work in collaboration with both Robert Adam and James Wyatt.

The Prince had married Mrs. Fitzherbert in 1785. At this period she accompanied him to Brighthelmston each year, and their happiest days were probably spent there. Mrs. Fitzherbert never actually slept at the Pavilion but always took a house of her own close by. In 1804 she commissioned William Porden to build her a house on the Steine immediately to the north of the first Marlborough House. Steine House, as it was called, took the place of a small lodging house belonging to a Quaker named Tuppen. It was occupied by Mrs. Fitzherbert until her death in 1837 and was throughout her life the foremost house in the town after the Pavilion. If the first half of the term 'patron saint' was unquestionably appropriate to George IV, the second half did not ill fit this much misused lady who, in Brighthelmston at least, even before his death, was always treated with almost royal honours. The existence of her marriage to George IV was finally emphasised by her tomb in St. John the Baptist's Roman Catholic Church, Bristol Road, designed by Carew, which shows three wedding rings on the third finger of her left hand.

Steine House still stands to-day but was disastrously re-fronted by the Y.M.C.A. in 1884. Behind this new facade, however, most of the main features of the house have been preserved, including two-thirds of the fine cast iron imitation bamboo staircase, up which the Earl of Barrymore rode a horse for a bet (Plate 18), the drawing room, extending the whole width of the house on the first floor, an excellent chimney-piece complete with its original tiles and overmantel in the dining room, and Mrs. Fitzherbert's oval oratory, though the wall coverings of this last have perished.

There has always been a legend, quite unsupported by fact, that Steine House was connected with the Pavilion by an underground passage. This probably arose in the sixties of the last century when, after the house had passed out of the hands of the County Court Judge, William Furner, who was its last occupant as a private house, a flight of stairs was discovered leading to a blocked cellar in the basement. This cellar may possibly have communicated with the brick sewer beneath the Steine in which the Wellsbourn was encased, but there is no foundation for the romantic theory that it had any connection with the Pavilion. The only underground passage leading from the Pavilion is that which connects with the Dome. This was constructed well after the Prince had put an end to his association with Mrs. Fitzherbert.

Returning to the Pavilion itself, the Prince decided about 1801 to enlarge the building. At his direction between 1801 and 1803 Holland added two small wings, making an angle of 45 degrees with the east front. These contained a dining room and an additional drawing room. At about this time the Prince was presented with several pieces of Chinese wallpaper. He had them put up in the gallery connecting the saloon with the new north-east wing and caused the whole of the interior to be re-decorated in the Chinese manner to conform with the gallery. The decorators who carried out the work were John Crase & Sons. In 1803 or 1804 the Prince commissioned William Porden, who at the same time was building Steine House for Mrs. Fitzherbert, to erect for him large Stables to the north-west, and a Riding House. The former—now known as the Dome—was completed by 1805 and the latter, which since 1868 has been known as the Corn Exchange, by 1808. Both had an Oriental or Hindu exterior. These buildings were erected upon part of the land purchased by the Prince in 1802, which had been the Promenade Grove.

He now found that the continuation of East Street north of its junction with North Street bisected his property and ran almost under the west windows of his house. He therefore obtained the permission of the Town Commissioners to close this road and in its place constructed another road further west, along the boundary of his property,

19 THE ROYAL PAVILION, WEST FRONT. *From a print after J. Cordwell*

20 ST. PETER'S CHURCH

21 ST. MARGARET'S CHURCH

22 ST. STEPHEN'S CHURCH, the Interior

which came to be known as New Road. Not until 1807 did the Prince purchase the actual ground on which the Pavilion itself had been built from Weltje's Executors, Weltje himself having died in 1800.

The building of the Stables and Riding House in Oriental style made the Prince feel thoroughly dissatisfied with the chaste classical elevations of Holland's Pavilion. The erection of the new buildings happened to coincide with the construction of a house named Sezincote in Gloucestershire, which the architect Samuel Pepys Cockerell was building in Hindu style for his brother Sir Charles Cockerell, a retired Indian nabob, while the grounds were laid out by Humphrey Repton. While Repton was still working at Sezincote, the Prince commanded Repton to advise him about the style of architecture most suitable for the Pavilion. Repton, with his head full of Sezincote and with the sight of the new Pavilion Stables in the foreground, unhesitatingly recommended the Hindu style. He produced a series of drawings for the transformation, principally of the grounds, but showing elevations of an orientalised building. The Prince pronounced them perfect and paid Repton for them, but curiously enough never used them.

The purchase of Marlborough House to the north of the Pavilion in 1812 provided the Regent, as the Prince had become the year before, with an excellent excuse for carrying out the reconstruction of the Pavilion, which he had been contemplating since 1805. How it came about that, instead of Repton, he employed John Nash who had once been in partnership with Repton but had quarrelled with him, has never been explained. But the Regent had first asked the Surveyor-General of the Office of Works, James Wyatt, to provide an estimate for re-building. If he had any intention of employing Wyatt to carry out the task, this was rendered impossible by Wyatt's sudden death in a carriage accident in 1813. But for this, we might perhaps have had a Gothic Pavilion at Brighton.

Nash began work in 1815. Marlborough House was demolished, and on the site the present Music Room was built. To balance this, a Banqueting Room was added at the south end of the east front. These rooms replaced the oblique wings added by Holland in 1801-1803. They had their tent-shaped spires and their Oriental façade of to-day, without the trellised verandas. Between them Holland's Pavilion remained intact, and its simple bowed façade provided a most incongruous appearance with the new Oriental box-like wings. However, during 1818 the remainder of the east front was brought into harmony with the wings and the verandas added (Plate 15). The north and west fronts followed in 1819 (Plate 19), so that by 1820 the exterior of the Pavilion had assumed the form in which we see it to-day. At the same time the underground passage was built connecting the Pavilion with the Stables. The only remaining addition was the conversion of the Ballroom of the Castle Hotel to the south-east intc the Royal Chapel in 1821.

Meanwhile, during the same years following 1815 the interior of the Pavilion was being re-decorated again in the Chinese style and for the most part with the wall hangings that exist to-day. The artists chiefly responsible for this work were Frederick Crase, Robert Jones and Lambelet. The Christian name of the last of these does not seem to be known, or, indeed, much about him except that he died in poverty. His most important work executed for the Regent comprised the wall paintings of the Music Room. In the Banqueting Room the main chandelier and the original wall paintings were designed by Robert Jones. But most of these paintings were removed by Queen Victoria in 1847. When the Pavilion was purchased by Brighton Corporation in 1850 the Corporation was fortunate in securing the services of Lambelet to paint fresh panels, not copies of the old ones, for this room. Most of the rest of the decoration, for which the original accounts exist, was carried out by Frederick Crase's firm of John Crase & Sons. The original furniture, stamped 'G. R. Pavilion', some of it designed by Henry Holland for the original building, and much made by Edward, Marsh and Tatham, was removed in 1847, and though some of it has made its way into private ownership (Plate 16), the majority of it is now in use at Buckingham Palace, as well as such fixtures as some of the chandeliers and almost all the original chimney-pieces.*

The transformation of the Pavilion was completed by 1823. The King was in residence during part of that year but only re-visited the Pavilion on two more occasions: during the winter of 1824-1825, and early in 1827. His final departure was on the 7th March, 1827. Like all the great builders of history, George IV was much more interested in the actual transformation of his various palaces than in the completion of the work concerned. When the result was achieved, he lost interest in it and began to think about further improvements. As he grew older he became less fond of Brighton, now a very different sort of resort from the small seaside town he had known in 1783 or even in 1800. As he came less and less to relish public appearances, the crowds in Brighton, which later so much annoyed Queen Victoria, grew larger each year. He began to find the seclusion of the Cottage at Windsor more and more attractive. Finally, it is said that the discovery of a remark offensive to Lady Conyngham, his last mistress, written with a diamond upon a window pane—or, according to another report, the word 'Unpaid' chalked upon one of the great mirrors in the Pavilion—decided the King to

*For details of the interior decoration of the Pavilion, and for its general history, the reader is referred to Mr. Henry D. Roberts's *History of the Royal Pavilion* and Mr. Clifford Musgrave's *The Royal Pavilion*.

leave Brighton for good. At all events, after 1827 he never returned.

The unpopularity of the King when Prince Regent, and the fact that the name Pavilion made a rhyming jingle with 'million' caused George IV's seaside residence to be looked upon by contemparies as at best a folly in doubtful taste. Almost all the comments of that date were unfavourable. Even Sydney Smith made it the subject of his least happy recorded witticism, and those who were not scathing about it felt that the expenditure of so much money upon a work, the general effect of which was little more than bizarre, was unjustified. The next generation was so much concerned with moral indignation at George IV's far from exemplary character that some of this over-spilled upon his building enterprises. Time has, however, corrected these inadequate judgments. The publication of the accounts relating to the Pavilion in Mr. Roberts's book showed that the total cost of all the different plots of land of which the estate was comprised, the construction of both Holland's and Nash's Pavilion, including the Stables and Riding House, the internal decoration and all the furniture made for the building, did not exceed half a million. It would probably be a safe conjecture that the original furniture and fittings preserved in Buckingham Palace alone would be worth nearly half this amount to-day. As for the building itself, purchased by Brighton Corporation in 1850 for £50,000, this must have been one of the cheapest and subsequently most profitable purchases on record. To-day it is in the fullest sense a national building, for which the usually much-overworked word 'unique' is entirely accurate. It has an interest and significance which reaches far beyond not only Brighton but even England. Though it is legally the property of Brighton Corporation and through them of the inhabitants of Brighton, of whom they are the corporate representatives, the latter should in fact be considered, as in the case of state ownership, trustees of this unique building for a community wider even than that of the nation.

CHAPTER SEVEN

The Regency

FOR THE FIRST fifty years of Brighthelmston's popularity no one seems to have thought that pleasure could be derived from looking at or walking by the sea. Until at least as late as 1810 the Steine remained the focal point of life in Brighton, as the town began to be called at about this time. Gradually buildings spread eastward. A lodging house in Madeira Place (until 1914 known as German Place) is mentioned as early as 1789. Manchester Street, Charles Street and Broad Street all date from about the turn of the century. No. 10 Manchester Street, built at this period, is one of the few houses in Brighton to retain its original curved shop front with glazing bars intact. Another better known shop of the same period is Cowley's Bun Shoppe in Pool Valley (Plate 3). This is dated 1794 and is still in the possession of the same family by whom the business was founded. A third is No. 6 Little East Street, now a private house called Andrew's Cottage after the last tenant of the shop, an old fisherman named Andrew, who for many years sold nets and all kinds of fishing tackle there. Dorset Gardens and Devonshire Place further east are mentioned in a Directory of 1809.

The first series of houses to be built actually facing the sea was Royal Crescent. This was begun in 1798 or 1799 and finished in 1807. It was built by a West Indian speculator named J. B. Otto. The houses are faced with black mathematical tiles, which are a special feature of seaside architecture and are seldom to be seen elsewhere (Plate 10). In the centre of the garden enclosure of the Crescent, Otto erected a buff-coloured plaster statue of the Prince of

Wales designed by Rossi and made in the Coade factory of artificial stone. This stood seven feet high on a pedestal 11 feet high carved with the inscription 'The Prince's Statue'. It showed the Prince dressed in the uniform of a Colonel of the Tenth Hussars. Otto's object in erecting it was said to be to ingratiate himself with the Prince and obtain admission to parties at the Pavilion. He was far from successful in this object, for the Prince considered the statue little better than a sculptural caricature. The sea air had a very bad effect upon its durability. The fingers of the left hand which was extended towards the sea, part of the nose, the whole of the right arm and some of the mantle broke off. The result of these mutilations was that short-sighted persons inevitably mistook the figure for that of Lord Nelson. The remains were, in fact, so unsightly, that in 1819 they were removed. Arising out of this action a public subscription was set on foot for the erection of a more worthy representation of the Regent. Three thousand guineas were subscribed, and in 1828 a replica in bronze by Sir Francis Chantrey of the marble statue of George IV, which stands at the head of the grand staircase in Windsor Castle, was erected on the Steine where the 1914-1918 War Memorial now stands. This statue was moved to its present site near the North Gate of the Royal Pavilion in 1922.

At about the same time as Royal Crescent was completed, Bedford Square at the west end of the town was begun. This and Russell Street were the first extensions of the town to the west beyond West Street. The building of Bedford Square lasted until about 1818. In that year Regency Square, between Bedford Square and West Street, was laid out. The owner of the land was a certain Joshua Flesher Hanson. The architect is unknown but was probably Amon Wilds senior, who was to undertake such extensive building operations in partnership with Charles

Augustus Busby after 1822, as will be seen in the next chapter, or perhaps Wilds and his son Amon Henry Wilds in conjunction. The houses are built of yellow brick with their ground floor stuccoed and rusticated (Plate 1). Most of them were completed during the ten years following 1818. Like Bedford Square and Royal Crescent, almost all had, at least on the ground and first floors, those charming little bow fronts with elegant ironwork balconies and hoods over the windows which are such a constant feature of the small Brighton houses of this period. A French visitor to the town a few years later commented that the balconies with their tent-shaped canopies of different colours were so often interlaced with roses and climbing plants that they gave the town something of the smiling aspect of an Indian city. No. 1 Regency Square, or St. Alban's House, is of rather different character from all the other houses in the Square and was not completed until 1830. It was occupied from 1830 to 1837 by Harriot Mellon, Duchess of St. Albans, who had one of the most romantic careers of the eighteenth century. She started life as a penniless player in an Irish theatrical company but in due course became a famous actress. As such she attracted the attention of and eventually married the elderly banker, Thomas Coutts, who was 42 years her senior. When he died in 1822 he left her his entire fortune of several millions. Five years later she married the ninth Duke of St. Albans who was 24 years younger than she. Both marriages were singularly happy. The Duchess died in 1837.

More or less contemporaneously with Regency Square the adjoining Russell Square, Cannon Place and St. Margaret's Place were built. St. Margaret's Church at the west end of the last of these was consecrated on the 26th December, 1824 (Plate 21). It was built as a Chapel of Ease under a private Act of Parliament by a banker-chemist - wine merchant - actor - newspaper-proprietor named Barnard Gregory and was called after his wife, Margaret Gregory, who laid the foundation stone. The architect was 'Mr. Clarke of London' and the builders Messrs. Cooper & Lynn of Brighton.

The extension of the town to the east and west made it essential to provide direct communication along the sea front from one end of Brighton to the other. Up till 1822, even within the confines of the old town, there was no road along the front between Middle Street and West Street. Carriages travelling westward had to turn up Middle Street, proceed along Middle Street Lane (now South Street) and then down West Street. In 1821 a public subscription was launched to make a roadway along this part of the front. This was opened by George IV in person in January 1822 and duly christened Kings Road. A sea wall was built from Ship Street to East Street in 1825. There was still no thoroughfare south of Pool Valley and the Albion Hotel. To provide such, the sea had to be repelled. Groynes were erected and the sea wall continued eastward. In December, 1829, the Grand Junction Road, as it was called, from East Street to Marine Parade, was opened. This then secured an uninterrupted carriageway from the extreme east to the extreme west end of the town, which became a very important feature of life in Brighton.

During these years, 1800-1820, the number of visitors was constantly increasing. The coach service had greatly improved. By 1810 the time taken in the journey from London had been reduced to eight hours; by 1813 to six hours, when for the first time a coach completed the journey to London and back on the same day. The time was destined to be still further reduced by 1830 to four hours ten minutes and by 1834 to three hours forty minutes, before the arrival of the railway superseded coach traffic altogether. But this was still to come. These improvements had been made possible by the introduction of vehicles of lighter design, by the new macadamised road surfaces, by the better breed of horses, by reducing the stages from 20 to ten miles for each relay of horses, and by the elimination of calls at every public house on the route. Passengers were now given no longer for their own refreshment than was taken in changing the horses and were then hustled back into the coach. Coaches made it a point of honour and rivalry between them to run to exact time. In 1815, fifty-two coaches ran daily to London and brought people down for 6s.

CHAPTER EIGHT

Municipal Government

IN THE EARLY YEARS of Brighthelmston's history the only authority which existed for the regulation of local affairs consisted of a body known as the Society or Fellowship of Twelve. This was made up of twelve of the 'ancientest, gravest and wisest inhabitants, eight fishermen and four landmen'. Out of and by them the High Constable and two Headboroughs, honorary officials who were responsible for maintaining law and order, were elected annually. By the end of the seventeenth century the Society of Twelve became extinct and the High Constable and Headboroughs were thereafter elected by a jury of inhabitants summoned by the Lord of the Hundred of Whalesbone (the Earl, later Marquess, of Abergavenny). In the daytime a Town Crier or Beadle in cocked hat and full regalia operated as a constable and overseer of the Parish books. This picturesque office fell into disuse in 1877, which is a matter of some regret. At night the 'Patrol' of two watchmen, or 'Old Charlies' as they were called, perambulated the town, one of them acting as bell-man to call the hours. The Overseers of the Poor Rate also acted as Collectors in an honorary capacity.

In 1761 the population of Brighthelmston was approximately 2,000. By 1786 it had risen to 3,600. The first official provision with regard to local government was made by an Act of Parliament of 1773 which set up a body of 64 Commissioners for the general regulation of the town. The first Commissioners were named in the Act itself and were themselves empowered to nominate persons to fill any vacancy in their numbers. The qualification for acting as a Commissioner was the ownership of property in the town to the annual value of not less than £10, or in the case of residents, the occupation of premises of the annual value of not less than £20.

The main functions of the Commissioners under this Act were to arrange for paving, lighting and cleansing the streets, for which they were empowered to levy a rate of not more than 3s. in the pound on the same basis as the Poor-rate. The provisions with regard to nuisances were rather more picturesquely worded than in the official jargon of modern legal documents. The wording used was: 'Any Hogstye, Necessary-house, Flesh, Dung, Carrion, Blood, Offal, Soil or Filth, Ashes, Cinders or Rubbish, or any other noisome Matter whatsoever that might be offensive to any of the inhabitants'—but not yet tripe-boiling, which seems to have appeared to the framers of all Conveyances of property in Brighton in the mid-nineteenth century an ever-present menace that must be prohibited at all costs. An old survival specially mentioned as illegal was the barbarous practice of cock-throwing, in which a cock was tied to a stake, or suspended across the street in an earthen vessel, and thrown at until disabled or killed in the first case, or the vessel was broken and the cock liberated in the second case.

For the special purpose of maintaining the groynes in front of Brighthelmston, which had been erected to prevent further erosion of the coast such as had overwhelmed the old town beneath the cliff, the Commissioners were authorised to levy a duty of sixpence a chaldron upon all coal landed on the beach within the Parish. It was to avoid this duty that when the Brighton Gas Light and Coke Company came into existence, its works were placed just beyond the eastern boundary of the Parish of Brighton, in the Parish of Rottingdean, and were later transferred to Portslade.

The meetings of the Commissioners were held either at the Castle or the Old Ship Hotel. In 1806 a special meeting was summoned at the Old Ship to consider a suggestion of the Prince of Wales to the effect that the town should be incorporated. The proposal was negatived. But four years later, the town having considerably expanded, further action was thought necessary. The population had increased by 1794 to 5,669, by 1801 to 7,339, and by 1811 to 12,012. In 1801 there were 1,282 houses in occupation in the town; in 1811, 2,777, and 80 in course of construction. More comprehensive powers were required than had been provided by the Act of 1773 to regulate the affairs of a town of this size, and a new Act was sought. The Act of 1810 increased the number of Commissioners from 64 to 100. Apart from certain persons such as the High Constable and the Vicar of Brighton who, by virtue of their official positions, were to act as Commissioners so long as they held their offices, it provided a more democratic method of selection. Vacancies in the number of Commissioners were to be filled by election, the qualification for voting being the payment of not less than £20 a year in King's taxes. The qualification for acting as a Commissioner was revised to comprise the ownership of property in the town to the annual value of not less than £50 plus the occupation of premises of the same minimum annual value. The Act entrusted the Commissioners with far more extensive powers for local government than just the paving, lighting and cleansing of the streets. They were, for instance, authorised to build a Town Hall; to nominate Inspectors of Weights and Measures; to appoint Directors and Guardians of the Poor for the control of the Workhouse; to license the operation of hackney coaches, sedan chairs and bathing machines; and to appoint watchmen, beadles and constables. To pay for all these services the maximum rate that might be levied annually was increased from 3s. to 4s. in the pound, and the maximum duty on coal from sixpence to three shillings a chaldron. Of the public vehicles licensed to operate in Brighton, the only one which need be mentioned is the light carriage known as a 'fly' or 'fly-by-night'. This had its origin in Brighton, and the name, if not the actual vehicle, passed thence into general use throughout the country in reference to a hired carriage or cab.

The watchmen appointed under the Act of 1810 were provided with batons, lanterns and rattles to give notice to one another of their need for assistance when on the track of an offender. They are said to have been most efficient in the apprehension of delinquents and rarely to have let a quarry escape them. But strangely enough at a later date, on the 13th March, 1844, the then Chief Constable, Henry Solomon, was murdered by a certain John Lawrence, though the murderer was caught and duly hanged. It is interesting to note that as late as 1830 in Brighton, and 1854 in the Brunswick Square Commissioners' District in Hove, the watchmen continued the old medieval practice of calling aloud the hours of the night and the state of the weather. Criminals when apprehended had at first to be taken to Lewes for trial, as there was no Magistrates' Court at Brighton. The first Petty Sessions were held in 1812 at the Old Ship Hotel. In 1822 they were removed to the New Inn in North Street, of which the name was changed to the Clarence Hotel in 1830 in compliment to William IV. A year later they were transferred to the old Town Hall attached to the Workhouse.

Between 1811 and 1821 the population of Brighton increased from 12,012 to 24,429, and the number of inhabited houses from 2,777 to 3,947. In the next ten years the population increased to 40,634, and the number of inhabited houses to 7,700. It was soon obvious that further municipal powers were required. The Brighton Town Act of 1825 duly superseded the Act of 1810. This was a far longer and more complicated measure than either of its predecessors, anticipating by some years the steady trend of municipal government to become more and more involved. The number of Commissioners was again increased, this time to 112, and membership 'ex-officio' was eliminated. Sixteen of the Commissioners were to retire annually, though they were eligible for re-election. The minimum qualification of a voter remained at the payment of £20 a year in King's taxes. But to this was added a proviso to the effect that those who were assessed to such taxes on property of the annual value of at least £50 would have two votes, and above that figure an extra vote, up to a maximum of six, for every further sum of £25 in annual value of the property which they possessed. The maximum amount of the annual rate for general purposes was not increased by this Act, but the addition of a special water rate of not more than 1s. 6d. in the pound annually was authorised.

One of the most important events which had occurred since the passing of the Act of 1810 had been the arrival of gas. The Brighton Gas Light & Coke Company had been formed in 1818-1819, despite the opposition of the inhabitants who, fearing explosions, had petitioned Parliament against the introduction of this new-fangled and dangerous invention, in much the same way as so many towns, including Oxford and Cambridge, were to oppose the introduction of the railway 20 years later. In this instance the Company overcame local opposition by giving a public display of the harmlessness of the new lighting in the form of a sign representing the Prince of Wales' feathers installed by them at their expense over a shoemaker's shop in East Street.

The Pavilion was first lit by gas in 1818. In 1824 gas lighting was installed in the streets of Brighton, which was one of the first towns in England to receive the advantage of this system, and in 1825 in the Brunswick Square Commissioners' District adjoining. The Act of 1825 consequently gave the Brighton Commissioners powers for the regulation of the supply of gas and nuisances arising from it. It is interesting to note that a French visitor who came to Brighton in 1827 commented that the new gas lighting in the streets rivalled the daylight in brightness. He also noted that when he made his way back from a ball at the Old Ship to his own hotel in Gloucester Place at three o'clock in the morning, he passed so many people on foot, on horseback and in carriages, that he doubted whether even Versailles in its former glory could ever have provided a spectacle of so much animation at such an hour of the night as Brighton then presented.

The Brighton Town Act of 1825 also contained the first instance in local annals of a town-planning provision. This laid down that all new streets should be at least 30 feet wide. Actually such regulations were very little required at this period, as the landowners and architects who laid out contemporary building estates almost invariably tried to give their streets the widest possible proportions in contrast to the cramped alleys of the Middle Ages. Finally, the Act of 1825 echoed that of 1810 in prohibiting thatched roofs in the town.

The Commissioners appointed by the Act of 1810 had not built a Town Hall, as they had been empowered by the Act to do, but occupied part of the building in Bartholomews used as the Workhouse. It was not until 1830 that a proper Town Hall was erected. The foundation stone was laid by Thomas Read Kemp, Joint Lord of the Manor of Brighton, on the 15th April. The building was originally intended to have the plan of a cross, but the south wing was never built. This missing portion might possibly have redeemed the design, but, as erected, it is a singularly

23 THE CHALYBEATE SPRING BUILDING
St. Ann's Well Gardens, Hove

24 THE WESTERN PAVILION, WESTERN TERRACE

25 ADELAIDE CRESCENT, HOVE, EAST SIDE

26 LEWES CRESCENT AND THE ESPLANADES, KEMP TOWN. *From a print by W. H. Mason*

unsatisfactory edifice. The architect who was successful in the public competition for the provision of the design was Thomas Cooper, who built the Bedford Hotel. It is curious that, of his two known major local works, one should be so lacking in distinction and the other such a very successful building. The competitors placed second and third according to the merit of their designs for the Town Hall were Clisby, the first Surveyor to the Brunswick Square Commissioners, and H. E. Kendall, Junior, the architect of the Kemp Town Slopes.

In the next two decades the population of Brighton increased to 46,661 and 65,573 respectively. About 1852 the question of incorporation again came to the fore but proved a very contentious matter. Its chief opponent was the Clerk to the Town Commissioners, the all-powerful Lewis Slight, who was called by his enemies at the time the 'King of Brighton'. He considered the proposal of incorporation a personal reflection upon himself. It was, however, passed at a town meeting, and the Charter of Incorporation was granted on the 1st April, 1854. The first Mayor of Brighton was Lieutenant Colonel John Fawsett. But better known was his successor, William Hallett, builder of St. John the Baptist's Roman Catholic Church, Bristol Road, and the Bristol Hotel (now Bristol Court), Marine Parade. He was also the first proprietor of the Kemp Town Brewery. Another well-known Mayor of the early days was Sir John Cordy Burrows, who held office in 1857 and 1858, and of whom a statue was erected in the Pavilion grounds opposite the main entrance of the building.

The municipal development of the town was carried one step further in 1888 when Brighton was made a County Borough. In 1927 its area was greatly extended to take in the villages of Patcham, Ovingdean and Rottingdean. 'Greater Brighton' as the whole was called was inaugurated by the present King and Queen when Duke and Duchess of York. On the 30th May, 1928 they unveiled one of the pylons on the London Road, designed by John L. Denman, which mark the northernmost boundary of the extended County Borough.

CHAPTER NINE

Wilds and Busby: The Squares and Crescents of Brighton

BRIGHTON has been so much associated with the Regency that this period is generally considered to be the heyday of its social and architectural development. The word Regency can be interpreted in the strict sense of the political Regency from 1811 to 1820, and also in the looser sense of the Regency style which extended to the whole of the first thirty or even forty years of the nineteenth century. Owing to the attention that has been concentrated upon the exploits of the Regent as a young man and the band of gay companions who then surrounded him, the significance of the first twenty years of the nineteenth century in Brighton's history has perhaps been exaggerated. To a certain extent socially, but to a still greater degree architecturally, it was the twenty years immediately succeeding that were the most outstanding in the history of the town. Not until the Regent had become King did the greatest architectural development begin, and the peak years of this growth were from 1822 to 1828. Five hundred houses were in course of erection during 1826 alone.

The two, or possibly three, men who were responsible for the construction of most of the best architectural units in Brighton and Hove comprised the Wilds and Busby partnership. Charles Augustus Busby was a young architect, born in 1788, who was the son of Dr. Thomas Busby, musician and author. He studied at the Royal Academy School of Drawing and at the age of twenty won the Academy's

Gold Medal. At this period he published two books of designs, one of Villas and Country Houses and one of Verandas, Chimney Pieces and other embellishments. In 1814 he went to America and remained there until 1821. While in the United States he published *An Essay on the Propulsion of Navigable Bodies.* On his return to England he established himself at Brighton and entered into partnership with an older architect named Amon Wilds.

Amon Wilds, who was born in 1762, was a Lewes man who had carried on business in that town as a builder in partnership with his son, Amon Henry Wilds, under the name of A. & H. Wilds. About 1815 father and son moved to Brighton and set up a similar business there which grew and prospered. Amongst other things they designed and built Richmond Terrace and Waterloo Place. How Amon Wilds came into contact with Busby is not known. Their partnership began in 1822. Whether it also included Amon Wilds's son is very doubtful, but probably this was not the case. At all events, he certainly executed work on his own during the existence of the partnership.

Wilds and Busbys' first important work in Brighton was to provide the design of a great new estate to the east of the town for Thomas Read Kemp, one of the Joint Lords of the Manor and, after the Lord Lieutenant of the County, the Earl of Egremont, the most important person in Brighton at that date. The foundations of Kemp Town were laid in May, 1823. The estate, as built, consists of two terraces facing the sea (Arundel and Chichester Terrace) with two wings of a Crescent (Lewes Crescent) opening out northwards from the inner ends of these terraces and joined by a large square (Sussex Square) consisting of three sides, of which the east and west sides are bisected by a road (Eastern Road) (Plates 28 and 29). Some idea of the size and scope of the estate can be gathered from the fact that the span of the crescent (840 feet) is 200 feet wider

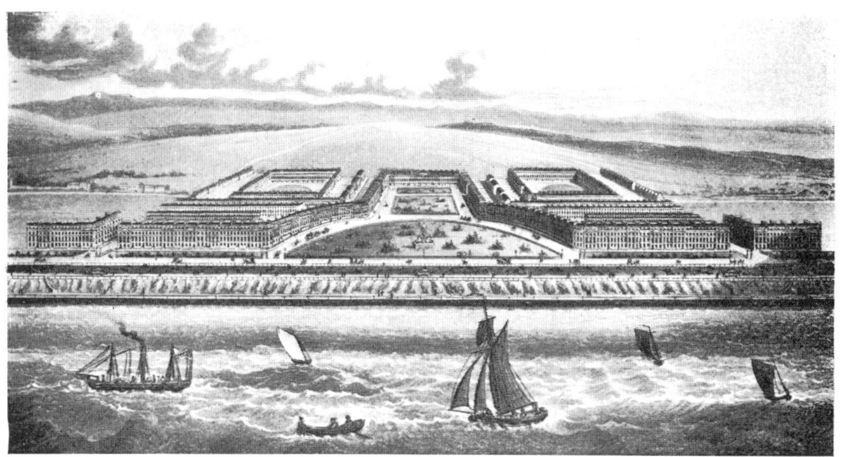

27 KEMP TOWN, showing the whole lay-out as planned but never executed. *From a print by J. Bruce*

28 SUSSEX SQUARE AND LEWES CRESCENT, KEMP TOWN

29 LEWES CRESCENT, KEMP TOWN, EAST SIDE

30 BRUNSWICK TERRACE, HOVE

31 BRUNSWICK SQUARE, HOVE, EAST SIDE

than that of the Royal Crescent at Bath. It is, in fact, in dimensions one of the largest estates in England conceived as a whole, perhaps only exceeded by the Nashs' metropolitan improvements in Regent's Park, then in progress and on which Kemp Town was almost certainly modelled. It was originally intended that Kemp Town should comprise more than double the number of houses actually built. It should have included two other squares, to the north of the terraces, and rows of smaller streets, probably mews, between. Plate 27 shows the original design for the whole. These additional portions were never built because Thomas Read Kemp's money was exhausted before the completion of what can be seen to-day.

The architects' share in the enterprise was limited to the provision of the design for the façades of the houses and of the general lay-out. The merits of the estate lie chiefly in the spaciousness of the lay-out—a splendid example of the unfettered scope of early nineteenth century town planning—as the design of the house façades is of the simplest, merely Corinthian pilasters fronting one house in three. Wilds and Busbys' plan of Kemp Town was exhibited in the Royal Academy Exhibition of 1825. The first portion of the estate to be completed was Arundel Terrace which, more than the remainder, was designed as a whole. The house at the east end now called Arundel House, which was originally the Bush Hotel, was licensed in September 1824 and occupied by June, 1826. All the façades of the houses (except Chichester Terrace) were finished by 1827, but most of them were mere shells. Their interiors were not completed until they were let or sold for occupation and were then designed on varying patterns to suit the ideas of their individual owners and constructed by different builders. The great builder Thomas Cubitt was responsible for erecting 37 out of the total of 106 houses. Apart from the Bush Hotel, the earliest case of residence was in February, 1826, when the centre house in Sussex Square, No. 25, was taken by Thomas Read Kemp's brother-in-law, Philip Laycock Storey. Kemp himself moved into No. 22 Sussex Square from the Temple, Montpelier Road, in October, 1827, and occupied the house for ten years.

The success of the estate at first hung fire. The reason for this has not been explained. It was not until the middle of the eighteen-forties that all doubts were removed as to the popularity of Kemp Town, and a few houses were even untenanted until the fifties. Meanwhile their carcases remained in scaffolding, as some old inhabitants of Brighton who died not long before the 1914-1918 War remembered them in their youth. Chichester Terrace was meanwhile confined to three houses at the east end and Chichester House at the west end. But about 1850 it was taken up by Thomas Cubitt, and the intervening space of 11 houses completed by him. In doing so he scrapped Wilds and Busbys' original design for the façades of the houses, which thus do not have the Corinthian pilasters of the rest of the estate, except the end houses that date from the original period of construction.

As soon as the proprietors of Kemp Town assumed control of their estate they decided to build a series of Slopes and Esplanades beneath the cliff to the south of Kemp Town (Plate 26), connected with the garden enclosure by means of a tunnel under Marine Parade. These were carried out between 1828 and 1840 and cost £8,400. Their architect was Henry Edward Kendall, Junior. In the centre of the upper terrace a building was inserted, comprising the entrance to the tunnel, flanked by two gardeners' cottages. Beneath this was a large room which was at first used as a Reading Room. The Kemp Town Slopes and Esplanades occupy a unique position in Brighton and Hove, possibly in any seaside town in England, in that they are the only portion of the sea front still substantially intact as originally designed in the first half of the nineteenth century. They remained in the use and control of the proprietors of Kemp Town until 1940 and were a delightful place of refuge in excellent condition until requisitioned for military occupation. They have suffered sadly during the war and since from wanton destruction. Brighton Corporation is now in process of taking them over and is to recondition them for public use. But their plans are first to be submitted to the Royal Fine Art Commission for the latter's approval.

Kemp Town has at different times had several residents of distinction. One of the first proprietors was the sixth, or Bachelor, Duke of Devonshire, who occupied No. 14 Chichester Terrace and No. 1 Lewes Crescent from 1829 to 1858. During this period he entertained many leading figures of the day at his house and in particular during the winter of 1848-9, gave a series of grand balls there which were outstanding in local annals. In 1896 the same two houses were taken by the Duke and Duchess of Fife or Princess Royal, as she became in 1901, and occupied by them until the Duke's death in 1912, and by the Princess until 1924. In February, 1908, King Edward VII spent a week there alone, and in May, 1914, Queen Alexandra stayed there with her daughter for three days.

Contemporary with the Duke of Devonshire's occupation of two houses on the estate, Nos. 19 and 20 Sussex Square were inhabited by the first Marquess of Bristol from 1831 to 1859. In 1850 the Marquess lent his house to Louis-Philippe, King of the French, who was then living in exile in England. The King spent a fortnight there with his family in April.

Amongst others, Thomas Cubitt occupied No. 13 Lewes Crescent from 1846 to 1855, and Harrison Ainsworth, No. 5 Arundel Terrace from 1853 to 1867.

As the Chapel of Ease for Kemp Town, Thomas Read Kemp built St. George's Church, which was erected in 1824-5. The architect was Charles Augustus Busby. At about the same time Busby was building the adjoining Portland Place. Bloomsbury Place, Marine Square and Eastern Terrace also belong to this period. Marine Square was constructed upon land belonging to William Attree, who was Clerk to the Town Commissioners for many years until 1825 and with this held so many other offices that, like Lewis Slight later, he was called by those who did not like him the 'King of Brighton'. He has left his most permanent mark upon the town in the shape of the very fine house, now the Xaverian College, which Sir Charles Barry designed for him in 1830 (Plate 32). This was intended to be the first of a series of similar houses encircling Queen's Park, but the others were never built. Apart from Marlborough House, Old Steine, it is probably the finest individual house standing in Brighton to-day. The small circular tower to the north-west of the house, now called the 'Pepper Box', was originally an ornamental building in the grounds known as the Observatory. The houses in Eastern Terrace are chiefly remarkable for very fine staircases, that in No. 1 (now the Court Royal Hotel) being probably the finest in Brighton (Plate 17). This house was occupied from 1876 to 1896 by Sir Albert Sassoon, who entertained the Shah of Persia there in 1889. The curious oriental building behind the house, at the corner of Paston Place and St. George's Road, that looks as if it was a piece of the Pavilion which has become detached from it, is the mausoleum erected by Sir Albert during his lifetime for his own tomb. He was buried there in 1896, and his son, Sir Edward Sassoon in 1912, but the bodies were removed in 1933 when the mausoleum was sold by his grandson, Sir Philip Sassoon.

While all this building was being carried out at the east end of the town, there was also much activity at the west end fronting the sea. Brighton then, as now, ended just to the west of what became Western Street and to the east of Waterloo Street. Beyond lay the parish of Hove, which at this time was only a very small village. Its population in 1801 was only 101 and in 1811, 312. In fact it consisted only of the Manor House—unfortunately demolished in 1936—and a few cottages clustered round it on the site of Hove Street. To the north-east was the Parish Church of St. Andrew, then almost in ruins. This was rebuilt by George Basevi in 1836.* After the commencement of Kemp Town, Wilds and Busbys' next important commission was the construction of a similar estate upon the land in the Parish of Hove immediately adjoining the Brighton boundary. This comprised Brunswick Square and Terrace and was at first, following the precedent of Kemp Town, called Brunswick Town. Work was begun in 1824 on the Terrace, and in 1825 on the Square. The three easternmost sections of the Terrace were completed by the end of 1826, and the Square soon afterwards. The latter originally consisted of 54 houses. Four were added later. At least two and probably all four of these additions were the houses with narrower frontages than the remainder (Nos. 7, 12, 47 and 52). They were squeezed into spaces which it had originally been intended to leave as passages through the sides of the Square. Such an afterthought was a great improvement, as two gaps on either side of a square of this size would have seriously detracted from the effect of the whole.

The fourth or westernmost section of Brunswick Terrace was not begun until 1827. Six houses in Brunswick Place below Western Road followed, and some of those at the

*St. Andrew's remained the Parish Church of Hove until 1892. The present Parish Church of All Saints', in the Drive, was designed by J. L. Pearson in 1889-1891. The chancel, transepts and chapel were added in 1901. Like St. Peter's, Brighton, mentioned on Page 77; it must be, for its interior, one of the finest Gothic Revival Churches in England, though of a later date, but the exterior needs its tower which has never been built.

southern end of the west side of Lansdowne Place, including Lansdowne Square.

This estate was on a smaller scale than Kemp Town. The whole effect is not nearly so impressive, though the façades of the houses have more architectural features. The Square lacks a central terminal feature, but the Terrace is a fine example of the 'processional' architecture, as John Summerson has called it, which Nash designed in Carlton House Terrace and the terraces round Regent's Park (Plates 30 and 31).

The most prominent part in the creation of Brunswick Town was played, not by the freeholder, the Rev. Thomas Scutt, but by Charles Augustus Busby, one of the architects. The houses were erected by different builders, but details of the plan and elevation were submitted to Busby for his approval. A copy of one of these specifications has recently come to light. It relates to one of the upper houses on the east side of Brunswick Square, but the exact number is not given. It was built for Charles Elliott, who was the first proprietor of St. Mary's Chapel of Ease, now St. Mary's Church. He was also the father of the first Perpetual Curate of St. Mary's, the Rev. Henry Venn Elliott, founder of St. Mary's Hall, and of the Rev. Edward Bishop Elliott, the second Vicar of St. Mark's Church. The drawing of the house, contained in a special green leather case, shows the elevation and ground plan with detailed measurements of the internal arrangement of each floor including the cellars beneath the road and the stables behind the house. It is dated 5th July, 1827 and signed by the builder, George William Sawyer and counter-signed by Busby. The complete price of the house 'papered, painted, with all Drains, Shores (*sic*) and Pavement' was to be £3,000. It is a most interesting document of the development of the estate.

It was originally intended that Brunswick Town should be self-supporting, and a series of small houses was therefore built in the angles of the Square and Terrace for the service of the main part of the estate. These comprised Brunswick Street East and West, Upper and Lower Market Street and Waterloo Street. To avoid the necessity for shops in the vicinity, a Market building was erected in 1828 between Upper and Lower Market Street. This became a riding school in 1839 and is now occupied by a firm of wholesale grocers. The Kerrison Arms Inn was also opened in the same year. This no longer exists. A Chapel of Ease of St. Andrew for the use of the estate was constructed in 1827-8. The architect was not Wilds and Busby, but Sir Charles Barry.

As Brunswick Town was outside the jurisdiction of the Town Commissioners of Brighton, its residents and their houses would have been subject to no authority other than the rather nebulous claims of the Overseers of the Poor-rate of Hove. To cover this deficiency a special Act of Parliament known as the Brunswick Square Act was obtained in 1830 which set up a body of 21 Commissioners entrusted with much the same powers as had been given to the Brighton Town Commissioners by their Act of 1825, for the regulation of affairs in Brunswick Town. This body became in due course the Hove Commissioners, subsequently Hove Corporation.

As far as occupants are concerned there is a distinction to be made between Brunswick Square and Brunswick Terrace. The former, from the beginning, was mostly given up to residents and some of these were of considerable interest, though not perhaps quite so distinguished as the most outstanding of Kemp Town. The Terrace, however, in its early days consisted very largely of furnished houses that were let to different tenants each season. Like all Brighton houses at that period they were let by the week and not by the month, in order, it was said, that the owners should gain one whole month's rent in the year. Rents in the town were extremely high during the season, and a French visitor commented that sometimes the amount paid for a single week was more than would be charged for a 'hotel' in the French sense of the word for a whole year in some French towns. Some of the visitors who took furnished houses in Brunswick Terrace in this way were people of considerable eminence and interest. Princess Lieven, for instance, stayed at No. 15 Brunswick Terrace in 1830. But the most important of these visitors was the great Austrian Chancellor, Prince Metternich who, while in exile in England after his fall from power, spent the winter of 1848-9 at No. 42 Brunswick Terrace (now the Alexandra Hotel). Here he had his celebrated meeting with Princess Lieven, who was staying at the Bedford Hotel that winter, after 26 years separation. Both were then old, and it was a far cry from the days of the Congress of Verona when they had been both political allies and lovers.

Returning to the architectural development of Brighton, during the period when the main activities of the Wilds and Busby partnership were concerned with Kemp Town and Brunswick Square and Terrace, Amon Wilds' son, Amon Henry Wilds, was busy with a smaller scheme near the western boundary of Brighton. An ambitious project for an Oriental Garden and a large glass building to be called the Anthæum had just proved abortive, and on the site of this projected garden Amon Henry Wilds erected Oriental Place and Sillwood Place to the north. He decorated the façades of some of the houses in Oriental Place with pilasters having the 'Ammonite' capitals with which his name is so much associated, and which he used in Hanover Crescent, Montpelier Crescent, Montpelier Road, Western Terrace, Preston Street and several individual houses in other parts of Brighton. These are called 'Ammonite' capitals from the resemblance of their volute to the geological fossil known as an ammonite, or whorled

32 THE ATTREE VILLA, now the Xaverian College, Queen's Park

33 MONTPELIER VILLAS, WEST SIDE

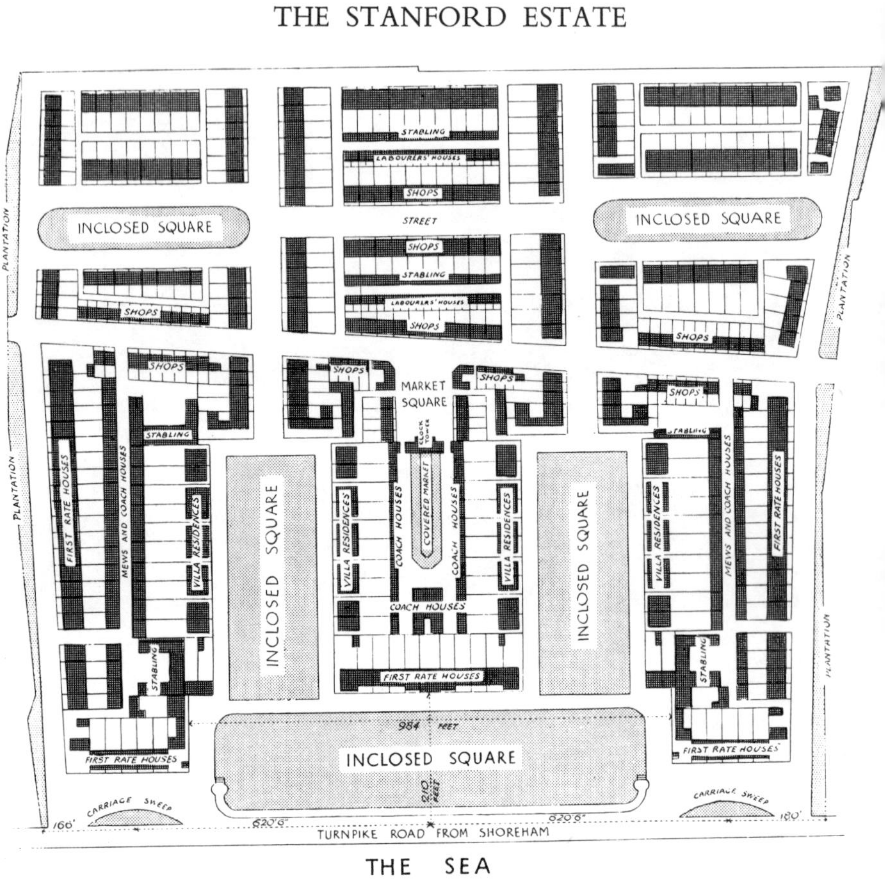

THE STANFORD ESTATE

34 Unexecuted plan by Sir Charles Barry, of an estate to be erected at Hove, for William Stanford, (*Redrawn by kind permission of the Royal Institute of British Architects, from the original plan in their possession*)

35 Elevation of the principal Square. (*Reproduced by kind permission of the Royal Institute of British Architects*)

chambered shell shaped like the horn of Jupiter Amon. For Sir David Scott, the owner of the land on which Oriental and Sillwood Place were built and a Director of the East India Company, Amon Henry Wilds built a large house named Sillwood House at the top of Sillwood Place. This is now the Sillwood Hall Hotel. Behind this building Amon Henry Wilds, acting on his own, erected a delightful little group of very small classical houses called Western Terrace, and for his own residence a single house in Oriental style with a dome on it. This last was called the Western Pavilion (Plate 24).

Amon Wilds, Senior, died in Brighton on the 12th September, 1833, aged 71 and is buried in the north-east corner of St. Nicholas's Churchyard, Brighton. His tomb, probably designed by his son and surmounted by a large shell decoration, is the most prominent in the whole cemetery. His partner, Charles Augustus Busby, died in Hove on the 18th September, 1833, aged 46 and was buried in the churchyard of the old Parish Church, Hove.

There remain two other constructions built during the reign of George IV that should be noticed. The first is St. Peter's Church at the north of the Valley Gardens. When the old Parish Church became inadequte for the accommodation of all the numerous visitors to the town, the first Chapel of Ease to be opened was the Chapel Royal in North Street. This was built in 1793-5 and was attended by the Prince of Wales until he took offence at a too outspoken remark from the pulpit which he construed as a personal allusion to himself. After this event he converted the Ballroom of the Castle Hotel into a private Chapel connected with the Pavilion. As the town became more and more popular, still further accommodation was needed for the fashionable company who wished to attend divine service. St. Peter's Church was therefore built as another Chapel of Ease in 1824-8. The architect was Sir Charles

Barry. This church, which is probably one of the finest churches of the early Gothic Revival in England, is splendidly sited with an excellent long view over the Valley Gardens, its elegant tower standing at the south end of the nave (Plate 20). St. Peter's was made into the Parish Church in 1873. The chancel by Somers Clarke was added in 1896–1902.

The only other structure of this period that need be mentioned is the Chain Pier which, for over seventy years, was such a well-known land and sea mark in Brighton. This was designed by Captain, later Sir Samuel, Brown, R.N., a naval officer who had served with distinction in the Napoleonic Wars. He was born in 1776 and went to sea at the age of 19, on board the *Assistance*. He served in this ship as Midshipman, Master's Mate and Lieutenant and then in 1801 was made First Lieutenant of the *Phoenix*. Ten years later he was promoted Commander but in 1812 accepted the rank of Retired Captain. He made a study of naval architecture and marine engineering and took out ten patents, one of which was for a method of manufacturing links for chain cables. This invention led to the introduction of chain cables into the Navy. Another of his patents was for the improvement of suspension bridges. In 1819-1820 he designed a suspension bridge across the Tweed near Berwick. He erected others at Newhaven, Leith, near Edinburgh and Heckham. He was knighted in 1838 and died in 1852.

The Chain Pier at Brighton was begun in September, 1822 and opened on the 15th October, 1823. It was hoped that George IV or one of the Royal Dukes would perform the opening ceremony. The Duke of Clarence was approached and returned a favourable though guarded reply. But when the time came no royal personage was present. The main purpose of the Pier was to provide a convenient place of embarkation and disembarkation for passengers travelling on the steam packets which were instituted at this period and plied weekly between Brighton and Dieppe. Previously the sailing packets had anchored at a point opposite to the coast between Ship Street and Middle Street. Passengers had been forced to put to sea in small boats known as 'punts', and their carriages and luggage had been shipped on board lashed to a raft. The new Pier enabled travellers to drive right to the ship's side. The charge for embarkation was £1 10s. 0d. per horse, £2 10s. 0d. for a two-wheeled carriage and £3 10s. 0d. for a four-wheeled carriage. The Pier stood opposite New Steine and was connected with Old Steine by a sea wall and esplanade extending as far as the present entrance to the Aquarium. The Pier itself consisted of four clumps of piles with a continuous suspension bridge between these, 350 yards long. The fourth clump of piles carried a T-shaped platform 80 feet wide which was the actual place of embarkation. Above each clump of piles were two hollow iron towers. In these were concealed small shops or stalls which were let by the Pier Company. The chains of the suspension bridge were attached to these towers and at the shore end were carried 54 feet into the cliff, where they were fixed to an iron plate weighing three tons. By the steps leading to New Steine were two cottages through which the chains actually passed into the cliff, and a Saloon, of which the great attraction was a camera obscura. At the head of the Pier beneath the upper platform were steps and galleries for embarkation when the tide was low, and on the north-east side a floating bath for the convenience of bathers. A piece of plate in commemoration of the opening of the Chain Pier was designed by Charles Augustus Busby and presented to Captain Brown. It took the form of a large cup or vase holding three gallons which was supported by the figures of three dolphins—the arms of Brighton. Round the sides was an engraved representation of the Pier itself. On the lid was a seated figure of Britannia encircled by two chains in allusion to Captain Brown's invention. The handles consisted of anchors. The cup cost £350 and was inscribed as a gift from the Commissioners, Inhabitants and Visitors of Brighton. It would be interesting to know what has become of this monumental vessel. Captain Brown left no issue, and it is probably reposing unused in the plate chest of some remote collateral descendant. The cup would be of very great interest in Brighton. It would be most suitable if it one day found its way into the Brighton Museum.

The Chain Pier rapidly became one of the most popular features of Brighton and its graceful silhouette was an artistic asset to the sea front in a way that the outline of neither of its neighbours of later date would allow them to be. A band played there once a week, and on special occasions displays of fireworks were given. It stood for 73 years and survived several severe storms. The first occurred on 24th November, 1824, and was called the Birthday storm. A picturesque print of it shows pedestrians' hats blowing in all directions and the billows driving against the Pier in great force (Plate 5). Another gale, on 15th October, 1833, inflicted considerable damage on the Pier. The third bridge was destroyed and the repairs cost £1,300. The Pier, however, survived until 1896, when on examination it was found that its head was six feet nine inches out of perpendicular. It was pronounced unsafe and closed on the 9th October. The end came two months later. During a severe storm on the night of the 4th-5th December, the whole structure collapsed with a great crash and disappeared from sight within a few seconds. The first clump of piles alone remained visible with its towers knocked sideways to an angle of 45 degrees. These were subsequently dismantled by a large crane, and all the remaining pieces of the Pier broken up and sold by auction.

The cottages and saloon at the shore end of the Pier, which in themselves were an attractive survival from the Brighton of George IV's day, were, alas, demolished in 1927 to make way for the Aquarium arcade. The only record of the Pier's existence to be seen on the spot to-day is a small brass plate attached to the iron railing on the south side of Madeira Drive which indicates where the Pier touched the shore. Brighton is the poorer for the loss of the Chain Pier.

NOTE

For further details concerning the Squares, Crescents and Terraces mentioned in this Chapter, the reader is referred to the author's *Fashionable Brighton 1820-1860.*

CHAPTER TEN

Brighton since 1830

THE DEATH of George IV did not have any profound effect upon life in Brighton, as he had not visited the town during the three preceding years. During the reign of his successor the Court continued to come to the Pavilion regularly every year. The new King was fond of Brighton and particularly liked to walk on the Chain Pier, which reminded him of what he called 'the most delightful place in the world—the deck of a ship'. He was wont to approach any stranger whom he saw there and begin a conversation with him. He was most unaffected and simple in his behaviour. For instance when driving he would put his head out of the carriage window to ask a passer-by the way, or if he noticed a friend would stop the carriage to ask if he could give him a lift. Queen Adelaide was fond of driving to Kemp Town to walk on the Esplanades, to the German Spa in Queen's Park—called after her—where imitation Carlsbad, Marienbad, Emms, Spa, Pyrmont and other waters were manufactured by Dr. Struve of Dresden, or to the Chalybeate Spring at the Wick, in what later became St. Ann's Well Gardens. A pleasant little classical building had been erected over this spring at the beginning of the century in the place of the temporary structure built by Dr. Russell (Plate 23). This little building was most unnecessarily demolished by Hove Corporation in 1934. The German Spa building still exists, though it is not in good condition. But it is still used in connection with the manufacture of table waters, by Hooper Struve, Ltd.

By this period the time of the Brighton season had changed. Sea bathing was no longer the main object of a visit. People came because it was the fashion and to take the air. The official season was from October to March, with a prologue and epilogue in September and April. The Court usually stayed from mid-November to mid-February. Life otherwise had not altered very much. The libraries and the Master of Ceremonies' subscription books still flourished. The theatre and, though to a less extent the races, still drew crowds. A new kind of diversion, or cure as the case may be, had recently come into existence with the introduction into England by the Indian Sake Deen Mahomed, of Turkish baths, or shampooing as they were then called. When undergoing the process the patient was enveloped in a sort of tent through which he was massaged by a pair of arms belonging to an invisible body outside. Mahomed's establishment, which was the first of its kind in the country, stood on the site of the west portion of the Queen's Hotel (Plate 13). Mahomed achieved considerable success with the treatment of rheumatism. His baths were hung with crutches left behind by the patients he had cured, as the votive chapels of the continent are decorated with naive paintings of the miracles which the saints of the chapels have brought about. Mahomed was in due course appointed Shampooing Surgeon to George IV and William IV and lived to the age of 102. On his death in 1851 he was buried in St. Nicholas's Churchyard between the church and the north wall of the churchyard. His establishment was absorbed in Brill's Baths in East Street which were also famous in their day.

The most popular, and at the same time the most fashionable, event of each day during the Brighton season was the carriage drive along the front from Kemp Town to Brunswick Square. Here the whole of Society congregated every afternoon in their handsome equipages to inhale the sea air and inspect the company. 'If I mount my little white nag and ride from Kemp Town to Brunswick Terrace', wrote Horace Smith, 'I am sure of half-a-dozen invitations to dinner,' which gives some idea of the nature of this parade. The most fashionable hotels were now the York, opened in 1819, the Albion, opened in 1826, and above all, the Bedford, opened in 1829, which received a very long list of distinguished visitors between 1830 and 1860. Charles Dickens is particularly associated with the Hotel, and some of his letters to the proprietor, Joseph Ellis, are preserved there. A tablet on the outside also records that he often stayed there. The Gloucester Hotel, Gloucester Place—not now standing—should also be mentioned. The Old Ship still flourished. But the Castle had been demolished in 1822.

The reform Act of 1832, which disenfranchised Shoreham, Bramber and Steyning among other places, allotted two members to Brighton. The first two candidates elected were Isaac Newton Wigney, a local banker, and George Faithful, a solicitor in the town. Wigney was returned again in 1835, this time in conjunction with Captain, later Admiral Sir George, Brooke Pechell, R.N., who continued to represent Brighton in the House of Commons until his death in 1860. He was the first occupant of Castle Goring, the house built by Shelley's eccentric grandfather for himself but never inhabited by him. Sir George Pechell's portrait hangs in the Brighton Art Gallery. Brighton was at this time a great Whig stronghold, and almost all its Members elected in early years belonged to the Whig party.

The main building enterprise of William IV's reign was the commencement of Adelaide Crescent, Hove, in 1830. The proprietor of the land was Sir Isaac Lyon Goldsmid, who also held the Portugese title of Baron de Goldsmid e da Palmeira. The architect was Decimus Burton, who was at this period designing for his father the new settlement near Hastings named St. Leonards, in which James Burton lost most of the money that he had made from his Bloomsbury enterprise. Ten houses were built on the east side of Adelaide Crescent, three facing the sea (Plate 25). But there the work stopped in 1834. Nothing further was done until about 1850. Why this was so, has never been explained. There was no question of lack of funds on the part of the proprietor as at Kemp Town. On the land to the north of the Crescent, now occupied by Palmeira Square, plans were made for the construction of a gigantic circular conservatory to be called the Anthæum which, if built, would have foreshadowed the Crystal Palace. But the iron framework, through faulty construction, collapsed before the glass was inserted, and the debris of twisted girders remained on the ground untouched for many years. It is said that at the time of the Great Exhibition, Joseph Paxton visited Brighton specially to see if any plans of this unlucky building were in existence which would be of assistance to him in the construction of the Crystal Palace. About 1850 Sir Isaac Goldsmid decided to finish Adelaide Crescent. But, though Decimus Burton was still alive, he was not employed to supervise the completion of the estate, and his original design appears to have been scrapped. Even the remaining houses on the east side of Adelaide Crescent are of much simpler elevation than the original ten, and the whole of the west side is of very inferior nature when compared with Burton's work. These houses were built between 1850 and 1860, and Palmeira Square adjoining between 1855 and 1870.

As the land on which Adelaide Crescent was built was outside the boundary of the Brunswick Square Commissioners' District, and Hove was still only a village a mile to the west, a second Act of Parliament was sought in 1851. This extended the Brunswick Square Commissioners' iurisdiction to cover all the land in Hove then being built on. In 1856 the Commissioners erected their own Town Hall in Brunswick Street West. When in 1873 the Brunswick Square Commissioners were transformed into the Hove Commissioners, the Brunswick Town Hall became the Hove Town Hall and continued to be used as such until the present Hove Town Hall was built in 1882. The old building is still standing and is now known as No. 64 Brunswick Street West. To complete the story of the municipal development of Hove it is only necessary to say that the Hove Commissioners in due course became Hove Corporation when a Charter of Incorporation was granted to the town in 1898.

The construction of Adelaide Crescent might well have been overshadowed by the erection of an estate of much ampler proportions on the land to the west of St. John's Road which was the property of William Stanford. A plan and elevations of such an estate on a gigantic scale have just come to light in the Royal Institute of British Architects, and my attention has most kindly been drawn to them by Mr. Marcus Whiffen. They are signed by Sir Charles Barry and are dated October, 1825, when the land on which Adelaide Crescent was subsequently built was in the hands of Thomas Read Kemp, who had bought it that year from the Rev. Thomas Scutt. Kemp had some intention of building an estate on it; but the erection of Kemp Town absorbed all his funds, and he resold the land to Sir Isaac Goldsmid in 1830.

The main feature of Barry's plan was a large square—without name—facing the sea and open on the south side. Even the north side which comprised the principal façade, was not made up of a solid block of houses for its whole length, but was flanked by the ends of two garden enclosures running endwise from the sea (Plate 34). The main square was very shallow, as the east and west sides only formed L pieces made up of two houses facing the sea and four houses facing inwards. At right angles to the south ends of these L pieces were two wings or terraces of six houses each facing the sea. In the centre of the square was a rectangular enclosed garden with a raised terrace forming a promenade. The main block of the square consisted of 12 houses of uniform size with a double-fronted house in the centre. The ground plan of each was made up of a dining room in front with a study behind and hall on one side of this leading to the staircase at the back. The drawing room on the first floor was only a single room and did not extend over the back room. The centre house had a breakfast room and library in front, with a drawing room over both, and a dining room and butler's room behind, the staircase being between the latter and the breakfast room. The design of the elevation was that of a Regency terrace blended with a considerable degree of Italianate influence, although the date was only 1825 (Plate 35). The first floor had continuous loggia balconies with a pierced stuccoed balustrade and round-headed arches over, flanked by Corinthian Capitals. The three centre houses and the end houses had Corinthian Columns rising through the first and second floors to support a modillion cornice above, and their top storey was not mansarded, in order to give slightly more height to these central and terminal features.

The two garden enclosures at right angles to the sea, which flanked the north façade of the main square, had on their east and west sides five pairs of semi-detached 'villa residences'. Between the inner rows of these were mews and in the very centre of the estate a covered market lit from a glass roof. At the north end of this was a Clock Tower looking on to a small 'Market Square'. On the outer side of the outer row of 'villa residences' were further mews.

In addition to the main square the only other 'first-rate houses' consisted of a single row facing outwards on the east and west flanks which formed the frame of the estate in these directions and looked on to a 'plantation'. These terraces or streets were separated from the inner rows of 'villa residences' by further mews. To the north of the squares which were surrounded by villas were still more stables. These completed the half of the estate south of what is now Church Road, Hove. This is marked on the plan as 'the road recently formed by Mr. Kemp', who then owned the adjoining land to the east.

The half of the estate north of this road is of clearly subordinate character to the other half. In the centre are eight parallel rows of buildings composed, in two groups, of rows of shops, 'labourers' houses', stables and shops. On each side of these are further shops forming a sort of square, north of which are small oval enclosed gardens. The whole is completed by two further squares, of which the character is not stated but which presumably were made up of houses of the second grade.

Why this magnificent estate never came to be built by William Stanford is not known. He did not die until nearly thirty years later, and the development of the Stanford estate took place after his death, with infinitely less satisfactory results from the architectural point of view. It is a matter of great regret that Barry's ambitious and imposing estate does not stand on the sight of First Avenue and its surrounding streets, which eventually came to be built by Sir James Knowles at the end of the nineteenth century. Hove is greatly the poorer by this unwelcome exchange.

Returning to Brighton, we find that after the death of William IV the tide of fashion still flowed thither every autumn. The young Queen was welcomed with enormous garlanded triumphal arches and at first took pleasure in her annual visits. These were continued after her marriage. Prince Albert found bathing agreeable. He and the Queen embarked from the Chain Pier on one occasion to visit Louis-Philippe. The royal children remained at the Pavilion during their parents' absence. But gradually the crowds, which had begun to displease George IV at the end of his life, became more troublesome and less discreet. They followed the Queen about, and *Punch* depicted them in full cry after her. In 1845 she paid her last visit and soon established her seaside home at Osborne, built, incidentally, by Thomas Cubitt who was responsible for the construction of so many of the houses at Kemp Town. The Pavilion was dismantled and in 1850 sold to Brighton Corporation for £50,000. Its formal opening as a public building took place in January, 1851.

The years 1840-1860 saw the erection of the last houses which had any suggestion of Regency character in their style. In most towns this style was exhausted by 1840, but in Brighton it lingered even later. The upper parts of Lansdowne Place and Brunswick Place, and Brunswick Road, all in Hove, belong to this period; and in Brighton, Percival Terrace, Clarendon Terrace, Eaton Place, Belgrave Place and the Montpelier Estate, including Belvedere Terrace and Powis Square. Montpelier Villas in particular in this estate is a delightful little street, built actually about 1845, but reminiscent of at least 25 years earlier in character (Plate 33). The very last group of houses in which can be seen anything of the grace of the stuccoed terrace of the first 30 years of the century, though blended with a vigorous but still healthy Victorianism, was Clifton Terrace, built about 1850. After this, building still continued, indeed multiplied, on every hand. The population for instance increased between 1851 and 1861 from 65,573 to 77,693. As Sir Osbert Sitwell and Miss Margaret Barton have said, the town 'became a victim of Victorian elephantiasis'. It would be difficult to claim that this development added anything to the architectural distinction of the town.

Socially, however, the second half of the nineteenth century in Brighton was a lively and colourful period. Although the Queen had departed, visitors were more numerous than ever. The older generation of royalty at first lingered on in the persons of the Duchess of Gloucester and the Duke of Cambridge. Foreign royalties, princes and statesmen abounded, especially during the revolutionary winter of 1848-9, which in some ways was the most successful season Brighton had ever known or was to know. The railway was opened in 1841 and by 1846 drove the coaches out of business. Six lines had competed for permission to serve Brighton. Sir John Rennie's, or the Direct Line as it was called, was the one selected. The branch line to Shoreham was opened on the 18th April, 1840, the main line to London just over a year later. The first train from London arrived on the 19th September, 1841, amidst great excitement. The fare to London was 14s. 6d. first class, 9s. 6d. second class. Day tickets were 20s. first and 15s. second class. The improved communications brought with them a stream of new visitors, not only in the winter season but in the summer for shorter periods. For the new visitors the West Pier was opened in 1866, the Aquarium in 1872 and the Palace Pier in 1898. But the celebrities were not lacking either, and until 1910 it would hardly be exaggerating to say that almost every famous figure in English life visited Brighton at least once.

During the reign of Edward VII, the King once more led the fashionable world on its visits to this famous seaside resort.

Of the years since 1914 it is perhaps too early to speak. They no doubt made their contribution both good and bad to Brighton's development. A striking example of each is to be found in Moulsecoomb, one of the earliest and one of the best Council housing estates in England,

and on the other hand in Western Road in which commercial tastelessness has done its worst.

The future will certainly bring with it plans for the erection of important new buildings. The construction of the new Town Hall, for instance, will be a splendid occasion to add to the architectural amenities of the town. It is to be hoped that the result will be as dignified and impressive as the new Town Hall at Worthing. But in any town that is as full, as is Brighton, of good architecture of previous periods, one of the most necessary concomitants of forethought for the future amenities of the town is the preservation of those architectural assets which already exist. It was with this end in view that the Regency Society of Brighton and Hove came into existence in December, 1945.

It is beyond question that the Royal Pavilion and the best examples of Regency and pre-Victorian architecture in Brighton and Hove, such as Kemp Town and Brunswick Square, not only are part of the architectural inheritance of England, which is and should be of interest to all informed citizens, but are also material assets of very considerable value. Since the War people have come to Brighton in large numbers to see these buildings, who would certainly have gone elsewhere, had they not existed. There is every evidence that such visitors will continue to come in large numbers if these buildings are given the protection that they deserve. Their preservation is therefore as much a matter of self-interest to Brighton and Hove as of public duty to the educated opinion within and beyond their borders. It is to be hoped that those whose function it is to control the developments of the future will ever be mindful of this two-fold responsibility for the historic buildings that lie within their care.

INDEX

INDEX

INDEX

INDEX

INDEX